BEACH BOUNTIFUL :
SOUTHEAST

**The Family Primer for Beaches
from Nags Head, North Carolina to Melbourne, Florida**

By Carol M. Williams

**With Original Drawings By
Sholar Ashworth**

D0325584

**Pegasus Medallion Press
Jacksonville Beach, Florida**

Beach Bountiful : Southeast

The Family Primer for Beaches
from Nags Head, North Carolina to Melbourne, Florida

By Carol M. Williams

 Published by:
Pegasus Medallion Press
P.O. Box 51404
Jacksonville Beach, FL 32240 U.S.A.

Publisher's Cataloging in Publication Data

Williams, Carol M.

Beach Bountiful: Southeast; The Family Primer for Beaches from Nags
Head, North Carolina to Melbourne, Florida / by
Carol M. Williams. -- 1st ed.

Bibliography: p.

Includes index.

     1. Seashore Biology -- Atlantic Coast [1. Seashore biology. 2. Marine animals. 3. Marine birds. 4. Marine plants] I. Title

2. Marine Fauna -- Atlantic Coast

ISBN 0-9636114-4-5 $ 14.95   Softcover   93-83639

FOR CATIE AND DAVID

"There are three schoolmasters for everybody that will employ them -- the senses, intelligent companions and books."

Henry Ward Beecher

Acknowledgments

Because I am a layperson, I relied on experts in the fields of marine science, ornithology, conchology and botany to help with specimen identification and to double check scientific information. Many thanks to Dr. Ted Allen, Patricia Raves, Dr. Kim Miller, Dr. Lillian Miller, Charlotte Lloyd and Mike Walker. My editor, Jo Ann Young, believed in the project and her advice and counsel were crucial. And much gratitude to all those who encouraged me to provide this tale and compendium for fellow beach lovers, young and old.

Table of Contents

PREFACE

Talk to any oldtimer in any beach community and he will, with great sadness, tell you that the good, old days of shell collecting are lost in the mists of time -- the days when you could find large conchs or sand dollars or elegant dosinia, just lying on the beach for the taking. And though the perception may be that our beaches have been ravaged by fishermen and shell collectors, the decline of choice shells awash on our beaches is primarily due to loss of habitat. The breeding grounds of marine animals have been destroyed by dredge and fill operations and pollution. In spite of these conditions, surprises still await the beach walker, and the relative scarcity of shells makes their discovery even more precious.

Most beach walkers conclude no moment spent on a beach is a wasted moment. And that perhaps has been my greatest reward for a year spent walking on southeastern beaches. No matter how barren the surface appeared, I never failed to find something I hadn't seen before.

The purpose of this book is to offer those rewards to the entire family, young and older. As you explore the beach, you will meet many of the life forms the beach harbors, some of them quite alien. But as even primitive peoples understood, to give an object a name is to extend a power over it and take a giant step toward understanding it.

With that proposal in mind, a few comments are in order:

* Identifications have been generally limited to shells, sea life, birds and plants that inhabit southeastern beaches;
* Line drawings by the author are offered of those specimens not shown in accompanying color plates; the intention was to provide a general configuration which would be helpful in identification;
* All names are in the vernacular. If you decide to become a serious student of marine sciences, there will be time aplenty to learn the Latin equivalencies;
* All measurements are apropos of adult or full-grown species;
* Italicized words are defined in the Glossary at the back of the volume.

And a word about Hap -- the pelican named Hap wanted to come along for the ride. And after you have met him, you will probably understand why it would have been impossible to turn him down.

A wonderful bird is the pelican,
His bill can hold more than his belican.
He can take in his beak
Food enough for a week,
But I'm damned if I see how the helican.
Dixon Lanier Merritt, 1910

Enjoy!!

Carol M. Williams
1993

Chapter One

Hap Introduces Himself

Just call me Hap!

That's what my friends call me. They just don't get into "Herman Aloysius." And can you blame them? But that's me, Herman Aloysius Pelican -- in fact, if you're on the beach right now, you can probably look up and see me, doing what I do best -- cruising the blue.

I know where the Herman came from -- that was my Dad's name. And that's alright, because my Dad was pretty neat. He was the practical one in the family. He could always find the best air currents and knew where our favorite fish would be. And friends tell me long before the rest of the clan got scared because so many of our eggs were breaking, he was hopping around on his soapbox, trying to get everybody riled up about something we were eating that was destroying our babies.

"Dad...hopping around on his soapbox..."

But Aloysius?   My Mom says she thinks it sounds distinguished; and you know how Moms are.   If it was good enough for a saint, it was good enough for her baby. I guess you might say she's the dreamer in the family -- always painting pretty word pictures about what's on the other side of the fence, up past our territory:

How nobly he struts his stuff in
The far North, this Atlantic Puffin.
His melodious voice, his regal bearing
As he pecks away at his dinner herring.

Cripes!!
Anyway, when my friends give me a hard time, I just tell them Aloysius is a right substantial name for a right substantial bird.   And just between you and me,

sometimes when I'm looking in the mirror, it's Aloysius I'm seeing, not Herman.

Well, anyway, you'll see me popping up from time to time telling you about this salty, sandy world of mine. I'll try to be practical like my Dad would have been, but if a little poetry slips in from time to time, try to ignore it.

"And just between you and me, sometimes when I'm looking in the mirror, it's Aloysius I'm seeing..."

Here about the beach I wander'd, nourishing a youth sublime
With the fairy tales of science and the long result of Time

Alfred, Lord Tennyson

Chapter Two

Meet the Eternal Beach

When you walk on a beach in the southeast, you see a shoreline of sand with a few instances of scattered rocks as at Fort Fisher, North Carolina and Marineland, Florida. The shore is restless and changing because the sand is constantly on the move.

Over the millions of years since the world began, the shoreline has moved inland and retreated seaward in a series of vast movements. As you stand on the beach today, the shore you see was shaped about 12,000 years ago when the last glaciers melted and the melting water caused the sea to start to rise. The rising sea gradually covered many miles of exposed beach, but this took thousands of years.

In fact, within the past 3 million years the location of the shoreline has changed at least a 100 miles in each direction. That means at some time in the distant past you might have gone to where Atlanta, Georgia is now and been at the seashore. Or maybe you would have driven to where

Jekyll Island stands today and still have 100 more miles to go before you could play in the waves.

And what about the sand - where did it come from? Wind and rain constantly erode the rocks and boulders you see lying all over the countryside. These fine particles of rock mix with clay and dirt. Then rivers wash and deposit them where the rivers meet the sea. This finely ground material is added to small particles of ground-up seashells. The whole mixture then is deposited on the shores all up and down the coast. The tiny particles of rocks and shells account for the gray and brown colors in the sand. The black specks usually come from a mineral called *magnetite* and the red usually comes from *garnet*.

That's Not All There Is To It

The beach may look like a barren waste of sand, dead shells, seaweed and discarded trash, but so much life lurks there. You don't see it right away because most of it is under the surface.

Early in the morning and just before sunset, ghost crabs flit across the sand to their holes. As the waves fall back into the ocean, small burrowing clams dig frantically into the wet sand to hide from birds and snails.

Just remember, under the sandy surface there is a whole, vast civilization that lives and thrives on this barren-looking shore. If you tune in to its rhythm, you can discover much of this life.

Hap's View of the Beach

Well, I guess that's how the shore was formed.   I wasn't here then.   But I don't think about that when I'm flying over the beach...and I bet you don't think about it when you're out there digging in the sand. You see lots of beach, of course.   And shells, water, grasses, blue sky and birds.   Most of all you see riding the waves, cooling off from hot summer sun, playing ball, building sand castles.

But I've lived here and maybe see it differently when I fly over the beach on my daily trips for food and fun.

Sometimes I see it as my dad explained it to me: "Herman," he'd say, "that's a big world down there and there are a million stories on that naked shore.   But the stories have one thing in common -- the constant struggle to survive.   Don't you know, each one of those shells is the remains of a life, a life spent building protection from enemies.   And the shells you see are the ones that lost the battle."

Well, of course he was right -- in his way.   But then my mom saw it through her rose-colored glasses. "Aloyisius," she'd say as she watched the beach from our nest overlooking the shore, "just look at all those beautiful shells; why, they're gifts from Mother Nature. Such colors!!   Like a master artist tipped over his paint pots on the sand and all the colors ran together.

"...those shells are gifts from Mother Nature."

"And see, some of them are on their faces with their backs hunched into the wind. When it's cold, it's like they're hunched up to protect themselves against the wind; but when it's hot it's like they're working on their suntans. And the ones turned over on their backs, filled with water, are making little offerings to us from the deep sea world."

That's my mom for you!

When To Search the Beach

Certainly the main contributor to the shore's rhythm is the tide which makes two full cycles in about a 24-hour period. Most of the burrowing beach animals follow the tide as it moves in and out; they depend on the seawater to bring them food and oxygen. Low tide reveals the most marine animals and shells, but a minus low tide, which is low tide during a full or new moon, is the absolute best time for a collector to be on the beach.

On any given day, there are two favorable times to look for live sea creatures. Nighttime is promising because most come out at night to feed when they are safer from *predators*. Always take a companion and a flashlight when searching at night.

Early morning is also favorable because the tide will have washed away traces of the previous day's activity. Then the beach's clean slate presents a clear record of the night's acitivity. Follow any trails in the sand and you could find a burrower's hiding place.

Shells litter almost every beach and they are there any time of the day. Of course, the lower the tide the more shells are visible. An especially good time to look for shells is two or three days after a storm which had a strong on-shore surf. The rough waters can dislodge more unusual specimens from deeper water and throw them onto the beach. Winter seas tend to be rougher than summer surf, also dislodging creatures and *detritus* from deeper waters.

Where To Look

Whether looking for live specimens or shells, to be most successful, begin by noticing certain beach characteristics. In general, the steeper the slope of the beach, the more energy the waves have when they reach the beach. This means they can carry larger and heavier shells. Energy-filled waves also tear more live shell animals from their deep water homes and deposit them on the beach. Waves running a long distance over a gentle slope, such as on the Georgia barrier islands, lose their energy before they get to the shore. Larger shells the waves might have been carrying drop long before they get to the beach. Scour both the high tide and low tide lines. Along the high tide line you will find bits of seaweed, shells of offshore species and other *detritus* from land and sea. It is along the low tide line you are most apt to find live animals in addition to the most recently-deposited, discarded shells.

Many southeastern beaches have been renourished with sand dredged from deep water, a mixed blessing. On the one hand, this manmade help often provides some interesting and more unusual shells for the collector; on the other hand, the dredging could have destroyed breeding and feeding grounds for nearby deep water species.

If you are looking for live creatures, coarse sand

beaches are more promising than beaches with fine sand. It is easier for clams and other burrowing creatures to dig in coarse sand because fine sand packs much harder.

Follow any trails or markings you might find on the sand, especially in the early morning. Snails often leave a silvery ribbon trail on the sand; also look for tunnels or small, sand hills. Such evidence might lead directly to where an olive or sand dollar has burrowed in the wet sand. Digging or raking the sand under these marks could reveal the mollusk.

Because oxygen penetrates less than a foot beneath the surface, deep burrowing animals depend on their *siphons* to breathe, collect food and eliminate wastes. Therefore, the depth of an animal's burrow depends on the length of its *siphon*, which must be able to stick out above the sand.

Bivalves, such as clams, leave different clues to their whereabouts. A depression or dimple in the sand deserves exploration. Check little holes, blisters and domes on the *intertidal* beach and in shallow water. You can often see their siphons sticking out of the wet sand. These are most visible where the tidal flow meets a flat portion of beach.

Don't overlook places where marine animals take refuge. Crabs dig holes in the dry sand above the high water mark. Be careful! Don't ever stick your hand in a hole. During the daytime, the crab is hiding in that hole and won't take kindly to being disturbed.

When rough water has washed seaweed onto the beach, pick it up and shake it over a light-colored towel or paper. Often live sea creatures take shelter in the seaweed. Check under rocks. Try raking or gently fanning the sand in shallow water to expose buried shells. Turn over barnacled planks to reveal any animals taking refuge. Break open sponges washed up on the beach. In the daytime, marooned sea animals will seek any shelter they can find.

Chapter Three

Shells and What They Can Tell You

Sit down on the sand close to some shells -- any shells. They are the remains of a *mollusk*. Most mollusks are soft-bodied animals which usually build shells to protect themselves from their natural enemies -- except for an animal like the octopus, which is an example of a mollusk that does not build an external shell but has its bony structure inside -- like human beings do.

Those marine animals that do build shells begin constructing their shells even before they hatch, and they continue to add new shell as long as they live.

Shells are made primarily of a mineral called *calcium carbonate* which is a salt present in the mollusks' blood. The bloodstream carries the salt to the *mantle*, a fleshy part of a mollusk's body which is similar to our skin.

In special glands in the mantle the mollusk mixes a liquid form of calcium carbonate with other minerals to produce a liquid shell mixture. The animal then secretes this liquid through pores in the edge of the mantle; the liquid solidifies quickly to form new shell.

Foods eaten by mollusks are responsible for the different colors in the original shells. These color-producing foods concentrate in certain cells called *pigment cells*. If these cells remain in the same place in the mantle, a stripe is formed in the shell. If the cell moves around, a zigzag or wavy pattern is created.

There Are Two Major Shell Families: Bivalves and Univalves

Bivalves

Pick up a shell at random and examine it. You have likely picked up the shell of a *bivalve*, a mollusk whose shell is really two shells hinged together. There are more bivalve shells lying around on southeast beaches than any other kind. The reason for this is probably that bivalves are the second largest group of mollusks, over 10,000 different living species, and every bivalve produces two shells.

When the animal inside was alive, the two halves of the shell were held together by one or two strong muscles called *adductor muscles*. Using these muscles the animal can push its shell open far enough for its *foot* to protrude and enable it to move around looking for food. Marine animals use the foot to burrow in the sand or to move across it. Some few bivalves move by rapidly snapping their shells shut and creating a jet of water that pushes them forward through the water.

From between the two shells of most species one or two *siphons* stick out. These allow the animal to connect to the outer world, bringing food into its body and eliminating wastes. But if danger lurks, the animal's muscles slam the shells shut for protection.

These two-shelled mollusks are called bi-valves because the Latin word for "two" is "bi." (That's why telescopes with two eyepieces are called binoculars and cycles with with two wheels are bicycles; cycles with one wheel are called unicycles because "uni" means "one.")

Hap on a unicycle wearing binoculars

The Exterior
The five keys to identifying bivalves are shape, external structure, internal structure, color and size.

Shell collectors rely on a small number of "shape" words when they discuss bivalve shells. Turn the shell in your hand and look at it from the exterior.

Another of Mom's Poems

Always a circle, never square
These shells that come in a pair.
Though I must admit
Sometimes they bulge a bit
To the sides or the bottom,
An oval become,
Heart-shaped
Or egg-shaped
Straight lines are rare.

In addition to the overall shape, a shell can be described as *concave, convex* or almost flat (compressed).

Bivalves have a *beak* at the top of the shell which can be seen from the outside. This is the pointed, first-formed part of the shell and resembles a bird's beak.

Radial Rib Structure   Concentric Rib Structure

The rest of the outside consists of ridges or ribs. Sometimes the ribs radiate from the beak, the top of the shell, extending to the bottom margin of the shell. In other bivalves, ridges follow a concentric or semi-circular pattern around the shell.

The Interior

The interior structure of the shell is also very revealing. The position of the beak along the top margin of the shell is important: central, forward or to the rear. Also, notice whether the beak points straight down or toward the front (*anterior*) or the rear (*posterior*) of the shell.

Below the beak is the *hinge* line where the two halves of the bivalve were originally joined. Some hinge lines have a row of teeth in them, others are flat and smooth with only one or two large teeth. Whether large or small, the teeth allow the shells to lock together.

Below the hinge line, in the rounded part of the shell, are one or more *muscle scars* on the side *margins*. This is where the *adductor muscles* were connected to the shell. The shape of the muscle scars can be important to identification -- some look like a leaf, some are more rounded like a footprint.

In many bivalves a line joins the two scars together. This line, the *pallial line*, is where the mantle muscles were connected to the shell. Sometimes this line connects the scars in an unbroken sweep, but often there is a jagged indentation or a rounded bulge in the line called the *pallial*

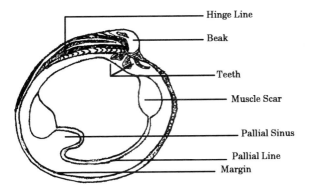

Hinge Line

Beak

Teeth

Muscle Scar

Pallial Sinus

Pallial Line

Margin

sinus. These could be considered the bivalve's fingerprints. Note them to aid identification.

Color and Size

Interior and exterior color can be important for identification purposes but they are not always reliable. Shells washed up on a beach often have taken on the color of the sand, mud or debris in which they were buried. Chemicals in the sediment change the original colors. Or if the shell has been lying on the beach for a long time, the color has probably faded and eroded.

Size can be misleading because shell animals fall prey to natural enemies at any time of their lives and at any stage of their growth. Maximum size can be useful in distinguishing between different shells, but remember that any shell will be smaller than adult size if the animal in it died when young.

ARK SHELL

Ark shells are among the most common shells found on southeastern beaches. They are strong shells, heavily ribbed, but not brightly colored though some have interesting patterns. The *hinge* line is quite straight. Their most distinguishing characteristic is their *taxodant teeth*, comb-like teeth that extend the full length of the hinge line. Different species have a different arrangement of these *taxodont* teeth.

Even when found on the beach, arks are often found with traces of a hairy *periostracum*. The margins are deeply scalloped.

BLOOD ARK. This square-like shell has 26-35 smooth, radiating ribs. Its *beak* is off-center but when still attached, they almost touch. The hinge line on the short side has a slight bulge at the bottom. This is one of the few *mollusks* that has red blood. 2"

INCONGROUS ARK. The very inflated shell is almost as long as it is high. It has 26-28 radiating ribs with barlike beads and a beak in the center of the hinge line. The hinge teeth are smaller in the center under the beak. 2"

PONDEROUS ARK. This very thick, heavy shell has 27-31 strong, radiating ribs. The *posterior*, or rear, margin is diagonally slanted down from the hinge area. The shell is often found with its thick, black periostracum except there is none on the beak. The beak is offcenter, very elevated and points to the rear. 2-2.5"

EARED ARK. This sturdy shell has 25-27 heavy, radiating, grooved ribs. The *anterior*, or front, end is short and rounded; the posterior, or rear, end is squarish. Young specimens have a noticeable wing or "ear" projecting from the posterior side. 2"

WHITE-BEARDED ARK. This small ark's many ribs are crossed by growth lines. The hinge line narrows in the middle and the interior is usually white. 1"

1. Incongrous Ark, interior 2. Blood Ark 3. Incongrous Ark, exterior
-- notice the *beading* 4. White-Bearded Ark 5. Eared Ark 6. Blood
Ark exterior with matching valve's beaks touching -- notice traces of
periostracum 7. Ponderous Ark

ARK SHELL -- Continued

ZEBRA ARK. This is a strong shell with red-brown, zebra-like stripes in a generally concentric pattern. The shell is much wider than tall and has numerous smooth, raditing, rounded ribs of irregular size. The *beak* is offcenter. When alive the animal has a series of eyespots along the *mantle* edge. 3"

TRANSVERSE ARK. This moderately inflated shell with its 30-35 radiating ribs is the smallest of the arks. There is some *beading* but found only on the left valve. The beak is offcenter and points toward the *anterior* (front). 1-1.5"

CUT-RIBBED ARK. This shell is large, moderately heavy with 30-38 coarse, radiating, grooved ribs. The beak is twisted anteriorally and the hinge line is perfectly straight. Fine concentric lines cross both ribs and the spaces between the ribs. 2-3.5"

MOSSY ARK. This irregularly contoured shell, also known as the turkey wing, is wider that it is tall. The exterior is irregularly criss-cross by concentric growth lines. The 6-8 posterior, radiating ribs are finely beaded and the beak is offcenter. It is often purplish-white inside and out. 2"

CARDITA

Carditas are not large but are heavily-ribbed *mollusks* which usually spin a *byssus*. None of the species has a *pallial sinus*, but some keep their eggs within a cavity inside the *mantle* instead of releasing them into the water.

NORTHERN CARDITA. This larger of the two carditas has a thick, fat, heart-shaped shell with 20 raised, slightly *beaded* ribs. Both the elevated *beak* and *hinge line* add to the overall triangular shape. 1.5"

THREE-TOOTHED CARDITA. This very small cardita's shell also has the triangular shape. The inflated shell has 15-18 strongly beaded, radial ribs. Notice how high above the top of the shell the beak is elevated. The bottom margins are deeply scalloped. 0.2"

MARSH CLAM

Marsh Clams are medium-sized with thick, inflated shells like carditas. They have small centrally located beaks that are not highly elevated. They live in brackish water and it is not unusual to see water birds making a meal of these delicacies.

FLORIDA MARSH CLAM. Its slightly triangular shell is thin but strong, and the hinge line has two large teeth below the beak. Concentric growth lines are widely spaced. Royal purple often tinges the interior or the margins. 1"

CAROLINA MARSH CLAM. This clam is rounder than its Florida cousin, and its atrong, inflated shell is usually eroded at the beak. The small pallial sinus at the *posterior* end angles slightly upward. 1.2"

DONAX CLAM

These colorful, small, wedge-shaped clams must be very social animals. Abundantly present on southeastern beaches, they live in large colonies just below the surface of the sand on the *intertidal* beaches. Their tidal wash ballet, combining both precision and chaos, delights the most practiced beach walker. Flawlessly, each one of the group moves in the same direction behind the wave wash -- if the tide is outgoing, they move toward the ocean following the receding wave; if the tide is incoming, they race landward, up the beach, after the wave has fallen back into the ocean. By instinct they know how to place themselves in the best position for the next wave to bring the most food. They can survive in dry sand for as long as three days. Beds of compacted, dead shells form a rock called coquina which has been mined in the south since colonial times. The most famous example of its use is in the outer walls of the Fort Castillo de San Marcos in St. Augustine, Florida.

FLORIDA COQUINA. Two sizes of coquina, very similar in appearance, live on southeastern beaches -- one very small and one larger. Their shells are sturdy with very fine concentric striations. Colors range from white to red with many variations in between. Colors are commonly rayed, in concentric bands or in a plaid pattern. 0.5" & 1"

Chef Hap's Speciality

DONAX BROTH

6 Qts Donax (makes 1 qt.)

Wash well. Don't quite cover with cold water. Bring slowly to boil. Stir occasionally after reaching boiling. Let simmer several minutes; stir twice. Drain immediately. Needs no salt. Serve chilled or hot with 2 tablespoons thin cream and small lump of butter.

--Cross Creek Cookery--

A variety of Donax clams; notice color and pattern variations and the holes in some valves indicating the *mollusk* was a victim of a snail.

VENUS CLAM

Possibly the most successful of all clams, Venus Clams have more *genera* and species than any other family of bivalves -- over 400 species world wide (and they are so easily confused). Their equal-sized valves are generally egg or heart-shaped and all have *beaks* that are off-center and point toward the *anterior* end. In all cases, the strong *hinge* curves up the top *posterior* margin in a gull-wing sweep. In most species three large teeth in the hinge lock the two valves together while the *mollusk* is alive. There are two *muscle scars* on the interior of each valve which are connected by a *pallial line* having a deep sinus.

NORTHERN QUAHOG OR HARDSHELL CLAM. In the past the Northern Quahog was prized by the Algonquin Indians as ornaments and money, the purple-spotted specimens being especially valuable. Today these large, heavy, moderately inflated mollusks are prized as good food. The shell has numerous, closely space, concentric growth lines except for a smooth space near the middle of the valve. 4"

SOUTHERN QUAHOG. The southern cousin of the Northern Quahog is larger, heavier and fatter, but it does not have the smooth area on the exterior. The interior is rarely stained with purple. 5"

IMPERIAL VENUS. This unusual, small shell sports 5-7 large, rounded, heavy, concentric ribs reminiscent of a woman's 1920's hairdo. The ribs are never thin or flattened at the ends. 1"

LADY-IN-WAITING VENUS. The sturdy Lady-in-Waiting is a whitish shell with many low, smooth, rounded, concentric ribs. Maybe she's been waiting too long because her ribs are wrinkled on the posterior end. The lower margin is *serrate*. The white interior is often stained with purple. 1"

CROSS-BARRED VENUS. This small, heavy Venus is fairly easy to recognize with its strong, raised, concentric ridges and many coarse, radial ribs. The posterior margin is longer than the anterior, and the white interior is often stained with purple. 1"

CALICO CLAM. This egg-shaped clam is easy to spot with its cream-colored, shiny, smooth exterior marked with brown, checkerboard design. The *pallial sinus* is quite large, often tinged with pink. 2-3"

DISK DOSINIA. These large, strong, circular clams are often found washed ashore with both valves still attached. They feel smooth because their fine concentric ridges are numerous and evenly-spaced. The deep pallial sinus is acutely angled. 2-3"

1. Disk Dosinia   2. Lady-in-Waiting Venus   3. Imperial Venus
4. Cross-Barred Venus   5. Calico Venus with snail hole at *apex* 6.
Calico Venus 7. Imperial Venus   8. Quahog interior; notice purple
stain, large teeth in hinge and muscle scar   9. Disk Dosinia
10. Quahog exterior

VENUS CLAM -- Continued

EMPRESS VENUS. This member of the royal Venus family resembles the Southern Quahog but is somewhat smaller with fine, radiating riblets crossing the raised concentric ribs. The *pallial sinus* is almost absent. 3"

GRAY PYGMY VENUS. The tiniest Venus clam is oblong with fine radial ribs crossed by concentric threads. The exterior is whitish-gray but the white interior is stained with purple at both ends of the hinge line and at the *posterior* end. 0.3"

SUNRAY VENUS. This Venus is smooth like the Calico but more elongated and larger. The exterior is marked with dark, radiating bands of color on a pinkish-gray background. 5"

ELEGANT DOSINIA. This cousin of the Disk Dosinia has wider ridges that are not as smooth to the touch. Its high *beak* also points anteriorally and the deep pallial sinus is acutely angled. As with its cousin, both valves, still attached, frequently wash ashore. 2-3''

LIGHTNING VENUS. This plump Venus is often confused with the Lady-in-Waiting. The exterior is crowded with prominent, concentric growth lines and mottled with brown markings. 1.5"

SEMELE CLAM

Semele Clams have circular shells which bulge slightly to a peak at the centrally-placed beak. Exterior colors are usually quite dull while interiors are glossy and colorful. The pallial sinus is well-rounded, bulging diagonally upward from the *posterior margin*. The live *mollusks* have quite long *siphons*.

WHITE ATLANTIC SEMELE. This medium-sized shell is usually dull white. The shells have numerous smooth, concentric growth lines. The interior is sometimes tinted yellowish or speckled with pink or purple. 1.5''

PURPLISH SEMELE. The Purplish Semele has a translucent shell that is thin but strong. Fine, evenly-spaced concentric, growth lines are crossed by fine, diagonal lines. The beak is sharp and pointed. The interior is glossy purple, brownish or orange. 1.3"

SCALLOP

Scallops, comprising about 250 species, are a readily identifiable family of *mollusk.* Several of the species are considered good food. The main identifying feature is the *"ear"* or wing on either end of the hinge line. The ears are about equal in size in most Atlantic Ocean scallops. The bottom (or right) valve is deeply *convex* while the left (or upper) valve is almost flat. Most shells have radiating ribs with deeply scalloped *margins.* Scallops are the least sedentary *bivalves* because they are good swimmers. They can move great distances rapidly by opening their valves and then snapping them shut, creating a jet of water to propel themselves through the water. All scallops have well-developed eyes along the *mantle* of the living animal. Each eye has a lens, retina and optic nerve.

ATLANTIC DEEP SEA SCALLOP. This large scallop is not often found south of North Carolina. Its rough exterior has flattened valves with many small, raised, threadlike, radiating ribs crossing the concentric growth lines. 8"

ROUGH SCALLOP. This sturdy scallop is rough, thanks to the 18-20 radiating, main ribs which are strongly *beaded.* Its hinge ears are very wide and of unequal size. The color ranges from yellow to red to bright brown. 1.5"

LION'S PAW. This unusual, heavy shell has 7-9 strong, radiating ribs with large, hollow nodes bulging from the ribs. The ribs also have numerous, smaller riblets. It is dark red or burnt orange and is a prized collector's item, especially if found intact. 3-4"

SENTIS SCALLOP. This is a dainty scallop with 50 fine, radiating ribs. The wings are of unequal size, the front wing being four to five times larger than the rear wing. 1"

ZIGZAG SCALLOP. The zigzag black lines on the flat upper valve make this scallop easy to identify. The bottom valve has 18-20 broad, widely-spaced, low radiating ribs. The interior of the upper valve is usually white, often with tinted margins. 3"

SCALLOP - Continued

ATLANTIC BAY SCALLOP. This subspecies, found on southeastern beaches, has 19-21 somewhat squarish, radiating ribs. The lower valve is commonly pure white and more *convex* than upper valve. 3''

CALICO SCALLOP. The valves of this scallop are easy to spot because they are so colorful, especially the upper one. Purple and deep red are the most common colors found flecked on the white shells. They have 19-21 squarish ribs crossed by concentric growth lines. 2''

RAVENEL'S SCALLOP. Don't get this scallop confused with the Zigzag. It has fewer ribs, about 25 compared with 35 on the Zigzag. The ribs are rounded on the flat upper valve and have wide spaces between ribs on the convex lower valve. The interior *margin* has a slight tint. 2"

Baby Hap on the half shell.
(Apologies to Botticelli.)

1. Ravenel's Scallop; uppermost valve is the top valve and is completely flat; adjoining it below the ears is the more inflated lower valve 2. Lower valve of Calico Scallop 3. Lower valve of a Calico Scallop 4. Upper valve of Calico Scallop 5. Atlantic Bay Scallop 6. Upper valve of Calico Scallop

JINGLE SHELL

Jingle Shells are thin, translucent clams. Because they lack *siphons*, they do not burrow in the sand or mud. Instead, through a large hole in the lower valve, the *mollusk* extends his *byssus* threads and connects itself to rocks, other shells or wood. The lower valve typically changes shape to conform to that of host shell and is seldom found intact on the beach. The upper valve, with no hole, is the shell commonly found on southeastern beaches. The upper valve, usually cup-shaped, has a single, large, footprint-shaped *muscle scar* in the middle. Rattling a handful of these shells causes a jingling sound -- hence the name. They are also called Mermaid's Toenails.

ATLANTIC JINGLE. Jingles come in a variety of shapes because their shape is determined by the outline of the object to which they were attached when alive. Though their tranlucency makes them appear fragile, they are actually strong. Color ranges from yellow-orange to copper-red to silver-black. 1''

JACKKNIFE CLAM

Jackknife Clams, or Razor Clams as they are also known, are elongate and narrow and the valves have sharp edges. The *beaks* are so insignificant as to be hardly noticeable. In spite of their awkward shape, they are the fastest digging clams and are agile swimmers. In fact, they can completely bury themselves in less than 7 seconds.

GREEN JACKKNIFE CLAM. This Jackknife has a thin shell with no curve. Adults are smaller than the Atlantic Jackknife. There is greenish cast to the *periostracum* if still intact on the shell. 2''

ATLANTIC JACKKNIFE CLAM. This is a long shell, moderately curved and not brightly colored. Its range does not often extend south of South Carolina. 6''

SMALL JACKKNIFE CLAM. The Small Jackknife is a very thin, fragile shell which can reach 4 inches long, but less than 1/2" wide. The shell is white with tan markings. 4"

At top and bottom -- Green Jackknife Clams with some green *periostracum* showing. On sides -- Green Jackknife Clams bare of any periostracum. Center -- a variety of Jingle Shells showing diversity of colors and shapes; notice the "footprint" of the muscle scar in the center of the center jingle shell

COCKLE

When you look at a cockle, it is obvious why they are called "heart clams" -- viewed from either end they are heart-shaped. These valentines from the sea belong to a large group of over 200 living species and are important commercially in Europe. Their valves are equal in size with *serrated* or scalloped *margins.* All have curved, strong *hinge* teeth and short *siphons.* The short siphons restrict the depth a Cockle can bury into sand. Cockles are quite active; they can even jump several inches by using their powerful foot. Most species are capable of changing sex.

YELLOW COCKLE. This cockle has a highly elevated beak which points almost straight down and twists slightly at the very point. The shell is strongly circular and inflated with 30-40 moderately scaled, radial ribs. It gets its name from its yellowish-white color which sometimes is decorated with brown specks. 1- 2''

COMMON EGG COCKLE. This egg cockle is larger than its cousin, the Morton Egg Cockle, but has a similar thin, polished smooth shell. The whitish exterior is speckled with brown, orange or purple and the small beak is not highly elevated. 1-2''

GIANT ATLANTIC COCKLE. The largest of the Atlantic coast cockles, the Giant Atlantic is a favorite for clam chowder. It has a large, heavy, inflated shell which is not as round as most cockles and 32-36 strong, somewhat rounded, radial ribs. The interior can be rose-colored but is always white at the margins. 4''

RAVENEL'S EGG COCKLE. Another of the egg cockles with a smooth, polished, inflated shell. It main difference is its more triangular shape which is sometimes marked with zigzag brown streaks. The center beak is small and not much elevated. The margins are slightly serrate. 1-2''

SPINY PAPER COCKLE. Another of the more fragile cockles, the Spiny Paper is compressed with about 12 low, slightly prickled, radiating ribs. The *posterior* margin is strongly toothed and the exterior color is often mottled. The small, center beak points straight down. 1.5''

STRAWBERRY COCKLE. This thick, strong shell has a sharply sloping posterior. The exterior has about 33-36 rounded, radial ribs and is checkered with brown to reddish-brown spots. The very elevated beak has a strong twist toward the posterior. 1''

1. Giant Atlantic Cockle; interior showing rose color   2. Spiny Paper Cockle 3. Common Egg Cockle, exterior   4. Ravenel's Egg Cockle, the typical pattern almost totally eroded 5. Yellow Cockle 6. Common Egg Cockle, interior; notice strong teeth on sides of hinge line 7. Giant Atlantic Cockle, exterior

COCKLE -- Continued

MORTON'S EGG COCKLE. This cockle gets its name from its thin, glossy shell. The small but strong shell, which is sometimes slightly pebbled, has no radiating ribs but does have concentric growth lines. The small, smooth *beak* is not highly elevated. 0.8"

PRICKLY COCKLE. The Prickly Cockle gets its name from its thin, well-inflated shell which has 27-31 deep, prickly, radiating ribs. It is less oval and more colorful inside than the Yellow Cockle. The very elevated, center beak points almost straight down, with only a slight twist toward *posterior* at the point. It is sometimes pure white, sometimes speckled with tan. 2.5"

THORNY OYSTER

Thorny Oysters are related to scallops but they have long spines and a ball and socket-type *hinge*. Like scallops, the hinge extends straight outward from the side margins into ears.

ATLANTIC THORNY OYSTER. This large *mollusk* has long, erect spines extending from various points along strong, radial ribs. The heavy shell is usually white but sometimes colored vivid purple, red or yellow. Any specimen found on the beach will probably be badly eroded. 3-5"

LIMA

Lima shells have many irregular, radiating ribs. The beak is not prominent on the hinge line. When alive, sticky tentacles protrude from the shell.

ROUGH LIMA. This large, pear-shaped shell has numerous radiating, barlike ribs. The ears are small but approximately the same size. There is a single depression in the center of hinge. 2"

LUCINE

Lucines are usually round and rather thick. Their shells are easy to recognize because of a long, narrow muscle scar at the *anterior* end of the shell and the absence of a *pallial sinus.* Their worm-shaped foot is six times longer than their shell. With the foot the clam manufactures a tube through which it inhales water.

BUTTERCUP LUCINE. The Buttercup has an inflated shell with fine concentric growth lines. The interior of the shell is usually flushed with orange and the exterior is a dull white. The *hinge* teeth are weak. 2"

CROSS-HATCHED LUCINE. This round, inflated, glossy white shell has parallel grooves running diagonally across the surface. Inner margins are finely scalloped. 0.7"

THICK LUCINE. This is a moderately heavy, rounded, yellowish-white shell with unequally spaced, rather sharp, concentric ridges. It has an obvious fold on the *posterior* end and a single strong tooth. 2"

WOVEN LUCINE. This small shell is almost circular. Fine radial and erect, concentric ribs form a criss-cross pattern. Shell margins are finely *serrated* and *beaded.* It is pure white. 0.4"

PENNSYLVANIAN LUCINE. This is a heavy, rounded, somewhat inflated shell. It has widely spaced, delicate, distinct concentric ridges and a deep fold from the beak to the posterior margin. Its small pointed *beak* is curved forward. 2"

FOUR-RIBBED LUCINE. Its four large, rounded, radial ribs give this lucine its name. It is a small shell, somewhat elongated and quite fat with numerous fine, concentric, squarish riblets. Margins are finely serrated. 0.3"

COSTATE LUCINE. The Costate is a small shell, usually circular and slightly inflated. Its fine radial riblets are crossed by finer concentric threads. 0.4"

DWARF TIGER LUCINE. Another tiny lucine, the Dwarf Tiger is a small, fat shell with strong, often divided, ribs crossed by concentric lines. 0.3"

LUCINE -- Continued

FLORIDA LUCINE. This lucine is common on southeastern beaches. Its moderately thick shell is much compressed with fine, concentric growth lines. Its rounded, very small, pointed *beak* curves forward. 1.5"

CHALKY BUTTERCUP. Though similar to the Buttercup, the Chalky Buttercup has a colorless interior. The exterior is white with concentric lines. 2"

BITTERSWEET CLAM

Bittersweet Clams are related to the arks. But these well-inflated shells differ in that their shells are oval and the *hinges* have fewer teeth. And instead of the straight hinge, the Bittersweet hinge is slightly curved. The beaks are central and somewhat elevated. The *posterior* muscle scar usually has a built-up, shelly ridge and there is no *pallial sinus.*

ATLANTIC BITTERSWEET. A silky look is created on this moderately large shell by its numerous weak ribs and fine radial and concentric scratches. The beak points straight down and the white shell is mottled with reddish-brown. 2"

COMB BITTERSWEET. This small shell has 20-40 well-rounded, radial ribs crossed by thread-like growth lines. The valves are of equal size and the central beak points straight down. The shell is gray splotched with brown. 1"

GIANT AMERICAN BITTERSWEET. The largest Bittersweet has low, rounded, radial ribs and the beak points straight down. The shell is not shiny, but dull gray or brown. 4"

SPECTRAL BITTERSWEET The smallest Bittersweet is more oval than round with a beak that points slightly toward the posterior end. It has weak radial ribs and a light brown color. 0.7"

1. Atlantic Bittersweet 2. Atlantic Bittersweet, interior; notice the taxodant teeth in hinge   3. Comb Bittersweet   4. Atlantic Bittersweet 5. Chalky Buttercup Lucine 6. Florida Lucine, exterior 7. Florida Lucine, interior 8. Chalky Buttercup Lucine

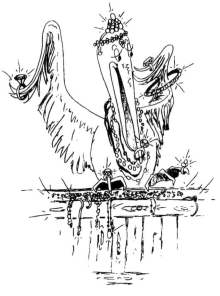

JEWEL BOX

Though not uncommon, Jewel Boxes are so unusual you feel as if you've found a treasure when you spot one. They are thick, heavy, unequal-sized shells which produce spinelike projections of varying length. The inner *margins* are finely scalloped. One of the valves, the larger and more *convex* one, attaches to rocks, corals, shells or other solid objects.

FLORIDA SPINY JEWEL BOX.   White inside and outside, these beach jewels are pitted with 7-9 rows of slender, tubular spines. The interior is often tinged with red or pink. Unique is the *anterior* margin line which bulges from the hinge line. 1.5"

LEAFY JEWEL BOX.   This Jewel has more numerous, large, scale-like projections with tiny radial lines covering the shell exterior. The inner margins are finely scalloped and the color varies from yellow and pink to rose. 2"

LITTLE CORRUGATED JEWEL BOX.   Not as showy as the other Jewels, this shell is small with low axial corrugations rather than long scales. The interior is white, sometimes tinged with pink. The inner margins are finely scalloped. These are often attached to pen shells. 1''

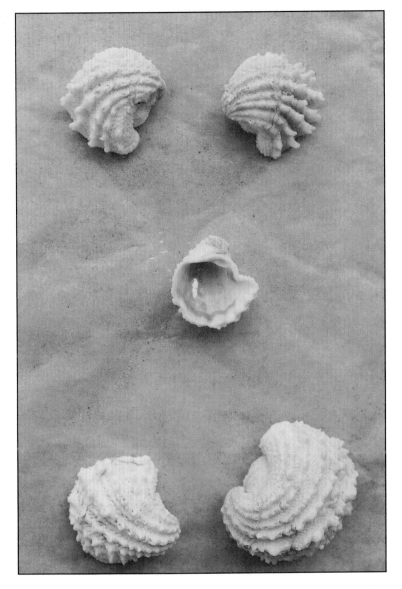

Florida Spiny Jewel Box; notice the spinelike projections on the exterior and the interior tinged with pink

ANGEL WING

Blessed is the beach walker who finds Angel Wings still attached. But don't be fooled by their apparent fragility. These clams, which have large, relatively thin shells, are capable of boring into wood, coral and moderately hard rocks.

ANGEL WING. This usually pure white shell, with its 26 well-developed radial ribs, also has concentric ridges which give a *beaded* appearance to the ribs. The *beak* is off center and the *hinge* line sweeps upward, especially at the *posterior* end above the beak. If it isn't broken off, there is a shelly, spoon-shaped structure hanging below the beak to which the muscles of the foot were attached. These *mollusks* can lie buried as much as three feet in the mud. Rare specimens are tinged with pink. 5''

CAMPECHE ANGEL WING. The most distinctive feature of this wing is the rolled-over plate and its approximately 12 distinct, supporting ribs which covers the *beak*. 3''

FALLEN ANGEL WING. This fragile shell, with its off-center beak and smooth hinge line, is identified by the shortened posterior end It also has a small, round indentation just below the beak and the exterior surface has radial and concentric wrinkles. 2"

FALSE ANGEL WING

False Angel Wings are clams of a different family than the Angel Wings described above. However, the False Angel Wing is also a borer into rock, coral and clay. Because of this, their shells are often deformred.

False Angel Wing. The chalky white, thin, elongated shell has many strong, radiating ribs and low scaly riblets on the inflated *anterior* end. Inside, the *pallial sinus* is deep and narrow. 2"

Atlantic Rupellaria. The strong, whitish-gray, usually oblong shell has many coarse ribs that are more narrow toward the anterior end. 1"

1. Angel Wing; notice rolled-over plate and barnacle remains
2. False Angel Wing, exterior 3. False Angel Wing, interior; notice
small beak and deep *pallial sinus* 4. False Angel Wing, exterior;
inflated anterior has radiating design 5. Angel Wing, exterior;
notice strong *beaded* effect 6. Campeche Angel Wing, exterior;
notice supporting ribs behind the plate covering the beak
7. Campeche Angel Wing, interior

EDIBLE OYSTER

Their value is for food and not for any pearls they may produce. You can spot these heavy, irregularly-shaped shells in great abundance on many beaches. When alive, they are usually attached by the lower valve to a solid object and remain fixed in one spot for life. Though the sexes in oysters remain separate, they commonly reverse sexes.

EASTERN OYSTER. This oyster has a large, rough, heavy shell, usually elongated and pear-shaped. The upper valve is smaller and flatter than the lower. The exterior is grayish, the interior white with purple muscle scar and purple at the margins. 3''

CRESTED OYSTER. The large, thick, oval-shaped shell tends to have a white exterior with pearly green to gray interior. Margins are coarsely serrate. 2-3''

An oyster from Kalamazoo,
Confessed he was feeling quite blue.
"For," said he, "as a rule,
When the weather turns cool,
I'm apt to get into a stew."

Anonymous

TREE OYSTER

Tree Oysters are related distantly to edible oysters but the family is important because they are producers of precious pearls, the only gem of animal origin. They produce nacre, or mother-of-pearl, which they deposit in layers around a grain of sand or any other small irritant which gets inside the shell. However, pearls from oysters in eastern waters are usually too small to be of any great value.

ATLANTIC WING OYSTER. This oyster has a moderately large shell with pronounced wings. The *posterior* wing is longer than the *anterior*. The left valve is inflated, the right value flattened. The exterior is dark brown and rough with a few pale rays. The interior is purplish-white. 2.5"

Top Left: Atlantic Wing Oyster, interior. Top Right: Atlantic Wing
Oyster, exterior. Middle Left: Common Eastern Oyster, eroded.
Middle Right: Common Eastern Oyster, interior. Bottom: Eastern
Oyster.

PEN SHELL

Pen shells, which are relatives of mussels, are large, thin, brittle, and triangularly-shaped. They have a straight *hinge* line and are usually a dark greenish-brown when found washed up on the beach. Many of the radiating ribs, of which the upper ones are quite large, bear erect, hollow, tubular spines. The spiny exterior makes an excellent surface for barnacles to fasten to. The interior has an irridescent lining.

The Pen Shell's small foot spins clumps of thin, horny material called a *byssus* which anchors the shell to rocks or other shells. The ancients spun the threads of the Mediterranean Pen Shell byssus into fine, gold cloth.

SAW-TOOTHED PEN SHELL. This pen   shell is very thin with over 30 ribs which have small scales. 6-10''

RIGID PEN SHELL. This wide pen shell, usually dark olive-brown, has 15 or more radial rows of tube-like spines on slightly elevated ribs. 6-10''

TRUE MUSSEL

Mussels are *mollusks* with strong, pear-shaped shells, a long hinge line, sharp *beaks* and shiny, usually blue-white interiors. Their valves are of equal size and are longer than they are wide. They excrete a ''webby'' byssus to anchor to roots, shells, etc. They can move to new locations by breaking the byssus and sending out new threads searching for a new anchor.

ATLANTIC RIBBED MUSSEL. This mussel has a large, thin, strong shell with numerous strong, radiating ribs and no hinge teeth. The exterior is yellowish-brown, the interior bluish-white. 3''

Top Left: Atlantic Ribbed Mussel, eroded.   Top Right: Atlantic Ribbed Mussel.   Bottom Left: Saw-Toothed Pen Shell.   Bottom Right: Rigid Pen Shell.

MUSSEL -- Continued

MAHOGANY DATE MUSSEL   This is a small, cigar-shaped shell. Each valve is divided diagonally by a sharp line and it is usually lime-encrusted, especially at the *posterior* end. 1''

EDIBLE BLUE MUSSEL   These mussels, commercially important in Europe, are found in crowded colonies attached to rocks or wharves. The moderately large, blue-black shell, some with radial rays, has thick, prominent, concentric growth lines and four small teeth under the *beak*.   The interior is pearly white or gray, becoming darker close to *margins*. 2''

TULIP MUSSEL.   Another moderately large, thin, strong shell, but the Tulip's color is usually a light brown, sometimes showing rose or light purple rays. The *anterior* end is narrow but the posterior is wide and has smooth, concentric, growth lines. The anterior beak is curved inward. A dull, white interior is sometimes stained with blue, rose or light brown. 1-2''

HOOKED MUSSEL.   This is a small, moderately thick, *mollusk* with triangular, curved valves.   It has numerous curved, radiating, whitish ribs and concentric growth lines and a sharply-curved beak at the anterior end.   Three or four small teeth are at the shell margin and the exterior is bluish-black. 1-1.5''

SCORCHED MUSSEL   This is a small elongated mollusk which is often found washed ashore attached to shells and seaweed. It has radial ribs which become more prominent toward the margins.   Two tiny, purplish teeth are at the anterior end. 0.7''

No, Hap, not "muscle" beach. It's mussel beach!

DIPLODON

Diplodons are small, roundish shells with small beaks that point slightly toward the *anterior* end. Each valve has two prominent teeth beneath the *beak* on the *hinge* line.

ATLANTIC DIPLODON. This is a small but strong, pure white shell with very fine concentric lines except at beaks. Concentric growth lines are widely spaced. 0.4"

PIMPLED DIPLODON. This delicate shell is chalky white with numerous concentric rows of very small pimples which give a *beaded* look. 0.4"

ASTARTE AND CRASSINELLA

The shells of both species are strong and heavy. They have strong teeth in the hinges and their shells are whitish to pinkish. Concentric growth bands are prominent and the *margins* of the valves are marked with tiny *serrations*. Since they have no *siphons*, there is no *pallial sinus* on the shells' interiors.

CRENATE ASTARTE. This small shell has approximately 15 concentric, evenly-spaced ridges. Its beak is often eroded and slightly turned toward the anterior end. 1"

LUNATE CRASSINELLA. This is a very small shell with a tiny, centrally located beak. The exterior has numerous, concentric growth ridges and the interior is usually brown. 0.2"

SPLENDID CRASSINELLA. This moderately large, thick, heavy shell has many closely packed, concentric ridges. The beak has no elevation. Manta Rays like to feed on this species. 2.5"

SANGUIN CLAM

Sanguin Clams are more readily found in warmer, tropical waters, but the Tagelus branch of the family will occasionally be found washed ashore on southern beaches. In Tagelus, the *beak* is very small though centrally located. Tagelus is much wider than it is tall, and they are almost rectangular. They have two small teeth in the *hinge* and a large *pallial sinus*.

STOUT TAGELUS. The Stout is a strong, smooth shell with fine concentric wrinkles. Discarded shells are usually white. 2.5''

PURPLISH TAGELUS. This fragile shell is smooth and shiny with a weak, radial rib inside each valve. The interior is often purple and the exterior can be purplish-gray. 1''

MACOMA CLAM

Macoma Clams are members of the Tellin family. However, their oval shells are usually dull white or chalky, never shiny like tellins.   The shell has a pronounced, *posterior* twist, and a large pallial sinus bulges upward from the bottom *margin*.

CONSTRICTED MACOMA. The posterior end of this moderately inflated shell is twisted to the right and narrows to a blunt end. The exterior has unevenly-spaced, smooth, concentric growth ridges. 2"

BALTHIC MACOMA. This medium-sized shell has unevenly-spaced, smooth growth ridges. The interior is 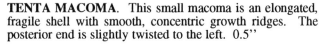 sometimes flushed with pink. 1''

TENTA MACOMA. This small macoma is an elongated, fragile shell with smooth, concentric growth ridges. The posterior end is slightly twisted to the left. 0.5''

Top: Constricted Macoma. Middle: Stout Tagelus, interior. Bottom: Stout Tagelus, exterior.

MACTRA SURF CLAM

Mactra Surf Clams have large, oval shells with a strong *hinge*. The *beaks* are elevated above a large spoon-shaped depression in the *hinge* line called a *chondrophore*. All types are marked by concentric growth lines or ridges.

ATLANTIC SURF CLAM. This clam has a smooth, large, oval shell with fine growth lines. The *pallial sinus* slopes slightly upward. In the Middle Atlantic states it is called the Beach Clam. 6"

CHANNELED DUCK CLAM. These clams are commonly found washed ashore. They have a thin, somewhat fragile shell with white or cream-colored, concentric ribs. They are a source of clams for clam chowder. 2.5"

COMMON RANGIA. The Rangia is a very sturdy shell, especially when compared with its cousin, the Channeled Duck Clam. It is grayish-white, very thick with a smooth interior. The beak is very elevated above the hinge line. The shells are used as a major source of road-bed material in the south. 2"

TELLIN

A Tellin is a nice break from the garden variety of shells. They belong to a very large family of *mollusks* which are usually colorful and very shiny. They are generally elongate in shape. Though the compressed shells vary in shape and size, you will spot their rounded *anterior* end and the slight twist at the *posterior* end with two small teeth in the hinge just under the beak. On the interior the *pallial sinus* scar is very large. They can burrow deeply into the sand because they feed through a long siphon which can be extended several times the length of the shell.

ALTERNATE TELLIN. This most commonly found tellin has a large, oblong shiny shell with numerous fine, evenly spaced, concentric growth lines. Usually the shell is cream or white, but sometimes pink or yellow. 3''

LINTEA TELLIN. Lintea is an all-white, slightly inflated tellin with many sharp, slightly raised, concentric lines. The pallial sinus bulges the width of the interior almost to the anterior *muscle scar*. 1"

1. Alternate Tellin 2. Alternate Tellin 3. Lintea Tellin, exterior
4. Lintea Tellin, interior 5. Alternate Tellin, interior; notice pallial
line and muscle scars 6. Atlantic Surf Clam, interior 7. Atlantic
Surf Clam, exterior 8. Common Rangia, interior 9. Common
Rangia, exterior 10. Channeled Duck Clam, exterior; notice strong
concentric ridges 11. Channeled Duck Clam, interior

TELLIN -- Continued

SPECKLED TELLIN. This tellin is not as shiny as the others. Its moderately large, elongate shell has many evenly-spaced, concentric growth lines. The small, sharp *beak* is slightly *posterior* of center. Usually the white shell has streaks of purplish brown. 2"

NORTHERN DWARF TELLIN. This tellin has the shine but not the size. It is very small and fragile and usually has fine concentric lines. Its iridescent color varies from white to rose. 0.5"

DEKAY'S DWARF TELLIN. Dekay's is similar to Northern Dwarf but more elongate and fatter. 0.5'

WHITE STRIGILLA. This is another of the wee tellins. Its small, oval, white shell shines and is criss-crossed with diagonal lines. The inner *margins* are smooth. 0.3"

CRENULATE TELLIN. The strong, thorn-like crenulations on the posterior end of this small, elongate shell are special in this species. The evenly-spaced, concentric ridges on this shell are somewhat sharp. 1"

FAUST TELLIN. This tellin is large and more inflated than some of the others. The smooth shell has fine concentric scratches and sometimes rather heavy, coarse growth lines. These tellins are a favorite food of the octopus. 3"

Univalves

Univalves, or snails, are a class of *mollusk* which produces only one shell for its protection. ("Uni" is the Latin prefix for "one," as in unicycle, which is a cycle with one wheel.) Even though the snail class, called *Gastropoda*, is the largest class of mollusks, containing over 40,000 living species, snail shells wash up on southeastern beaches in far fewer numbers than the *bivalves*. Each marine animal produces only one shell and most are more fragile than their bivalve cousins. Also, many of these species are less accessible because they live in deep water rather than burrow on the beach. Because many are quite small, they are difficult to see lying on the beach amid many other shells

Most snails are identified by a single shell, which is usually coiled or cap-like, a distinct head and a solelike foot adapted for creeping. This foot spreads out beneath the snail's body and makes a rippling motion that moves the snail forward. If danger threatens, the snail withdraws into the shell and a lid-like part called an *operculum* closes the shell opening.

Gastropods eat small clams, as many as three or four a day, by piercing the clam shell. They do this with their *radula* after secreting an acid which softens a spot on the shell allowing the radula to bore a hole through the shell. Notice, many bivalve shells on the beach have little round holes which are evidence they became a gastropod's dinner.

Exterior

The keys to identifying univalve shells are mostly external: shell shape, sculpture and, to a lesser degree, color.

Instead of a *beak*, a snail shell has an *apex* which is the first-formed part of a univalve shell. From this point, a snail creates *whorls*, round structures which either coil around a central axis, usually getting larger in diameter as they grow, or form ribs on each whorl which lie parallel to the axis.

The size and shape of the whorls is significant. If the shell is coiled, it will have several *whorls*, or coils and they will be joined to each other by a *suture*. The types of whorl and suture and the sculpture pattern on each will aid in identification. If the sculpture pattern is *axial*, the ribs lie parallel to the length of the shell and connect the sutures. If the pattern is spiral, ribs or concentric lines lie parallel to the suture lines. If the pattern is composed of strong spiral ridges, these are called *cords*.

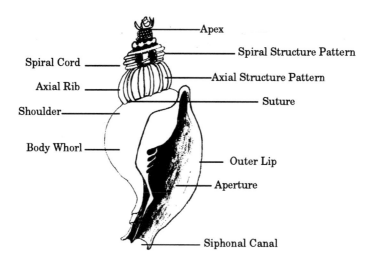

TRIVIA

Trivias resemble Cowries but are generally smaller and have small ribs which run around the shell from the narrow *aperture* to the center of the back.

MALTBIE'S TRIVIA. The shell is quite round but flattened above. 24-28 riblets cross the outer lip, and there is a shallow groove on top of the shell. The area between riblets is slightly granular. 0.4"

LITTLE WHITE TRIVIA. This very small, all white shell has 17-24 riblets and no groove on top. 0.2"

MAUGER'S ERATO. The thickened outer lip of this very small, glossy shell has 10-15 tiny teeth. The *apex* is pointed and the *body whorl* bulges more at the top than bottom. 3mm.

COWRIE

Cowries have highly polished, colorful shells. They are oval-shaped and have a thick-lipped aperture with teeth on both sides. Immature species are fragile, lack a curled lip and are usually banded. Mature specimens are usually spotted. They are not common north of the tropics. Cowrie's were used by primitive peoples as money and were evidently brought to this country by early fur traders because they have been found in the burial grounds of native Americans.

ATLANTIC YELLOW COWRIE. This relatively small shell is flattened on top and usually speckled with orange-brown or white. The base and teeth are ivory-white. Look for small indentations which occur where the top of the shell meets the rolled up lip of the aperture. 1"

ATLANTIC DEER COWRIE. The dark brown shell has small whitish dots and the teeth in the aperture are brown. These specimens are rock-dwelling and nocturnal feeders and can be found around jetties and other rock formations. 6"

SLIPPER SHELL

Slipper Shells, one of the most common *univalves* on southeastern beaches, are medium-sized, usually cup-shaped shells with a shelly platform on the underside. When you look at the interior, you will see the resemblance to a bedroom slipper. Young slippers move about, but older specimens remain attached, usually to another shell. In fact, slippers often attach themselves to each other in a tower arrangement. They are capable of changing sex as they grow.

EASTERN WHITE SLIPPER SHELL. These shells are generally white inside and out. The shape varies but is most often *concave* because these slippers often grow inside an empty snail shell and conform to the concave shape of the shell. 1''

COMMON ATLANTIC SLIPPER SHELL. This strongly arched, *convex* light-colored shell has flecks of light brown spots. In the interior a buff-colored shelf covers almost one-half of shell. 1.5''

CONVEX SLIPPER SHELL. A very small, reddish-brown shell, this slipper has a strongly arched shell. The *apex* is strongly hooked. 0.5''

CUP-AND-SAUCER SHELL

Cup-and-Saucer Shells are relatively small, rounded, cone-shaped shells with an apex that usually tips over slightly. A shelly "cup" is attached to the interior or underside of the shell which supports some of the soft parts of the snail when it is alive.

STRIATE CUP-AND-SAUCER. The base is circular with a smooth apex which is near the center of the top and tipped to one side. The exterior has small, wavy, spiral cords. The interior is glossy with a white, shelly cup. 1"

CIRCULAR CUP-AND-SAUCER. This is a very small shell with a circular base. The apex is central and slightly coiled. The interior cup is large with a thickened edge. 0.5"

Top picture: Eastern White Slipper Shells growing inside *aperture* of a discarded moon snail.   Bottom picture: outer ring of Common Atlantic Slipper Shells; Eastern White Slipper Shells in the middle; notice the shelf visible on the interior views

JANTHINA SNAIL

Janthina Snails belong to a family of relatively small, fragile, purple snails which live on the open sea usually floating on a mass of bubbles. They are sometimes blown ashore in great numbers.

COMMON JANTHINA. These are low-spired shells with slightly angular *whorls*. They are light purple above periphery; a deeper purple below. The *aperture* flares considerably. They can be more commonly found after storms in late Spring. 1''

ELONGATE JANTHINA. This low-spired shell has rounded whorls and well-marked *sutures*. It is not as flattened as Common Janthina and the purple color is more uniform. The outer lip has a distinct flare and the base of the aperture has a slight projection at end of *columella*. 1''

PALLID JANTHINA. Pallid Janthina is paler than its cousins. It has a low spire and is quite round. The base of aperture is also quite round but it lacks the projection found in Elongate Janthina. 1''

SUNDIAL

Sundials are small shells with a wide *umbilicus* which is open all the way to the *apex* inside the shell. The coils are wide but the shell is not very elevated.

ATLANTIC MODULUS. This is not a true sundial but is shaped very similarly. The small, sturdy shell has a flattened, low spire and shoulder. The base has five strong, spiral cords. 0.5''

COMMON SUNDIAL. This moderately large, circular shell has four or five heavy, somewhat *beaded*, spiral cords. The umbilicus is bordered by a strong, spiral cord. 1.5''

TOP SHELL

Top shells are finely sculptured, cone-shaped shells which are made of an iridescent mother-of-pearl inside and outside. However, the exterior mother-of-pearl is usually concealed by other coloration.

SCULPTURED TOP SHELL. This is a small, strong shell with a tall *spire.* The *whorls* have six major, *beaded cords.* The shell is light, usually mottled with splashes of red and brown. 0.8"

JUJUBE TOP SHELL. This rather small shell has 9-10, beaded cords between the *sutures.* The shell has a tall spire and is a brown to reddish-brown color with white specks above the sutures. 1"

DALL'S DWARF GAZA. This very small, glossy shell is smooth except for very tiny pimples below the suture lines. The shell has a flat spire and angular whorls which are gray with zigzag, brown stripes on top. 0.3"

CHANNELED SOLARELLE. This thick, whitish shell has a channeled suture. Whorls have six spiral cords; the upper three are beaded. The aperture is pearly. 0.4"

CONE SHELL

Cone shells are solid and cone-shaped with a long *aperture.* Exteriors are generally vividly-colored and decorated with a variety of patterns. Cones feed at night, particularly at low tide. They are interesting because all species have a poison capability with which they stun their prey. Because of this, large specimens should be handled with care.

FLORIDA CONE. This medium-sized, heavy shell has an elevated spire, sharp *apex* and pronounced suture. The whorls taper with tops of whorls in the spire slightly *concave.* The color is often white with wide axial patches of orange or yellow and white spiral band on body whorl. 1''

STEARN'S CONE. This small, slender shell has rounded whorls with spiral scratches in the spiral. It Is a mottled color. 0.4''

MOON SNAIL

Moon snails have a low spire and a wide *body whorl*. The large foot of the *mollusk*, which is 3 times larger than the shell when fully extended, is large enough to conceal the entire shell. Moon snails eat small clams, as many as three or four a day, by piercing the clam shell. Snails are able to penetrate hard shell with a combination of chemical and physical force. First they secrete an acid which softens a spot on the prey's shell. Then, with their *radula*, they bore a hole through the shell. You will notice many *bivalve* shells with little, round holes which are evidence they became a snail's dinner.

When they lay their eggs, Moon Snails protect them with a protective "sand collar" formed when the eggs are deposited. The snail creates the sand collar by mixing sand with a chemical it secretes. When the sand collar dries, it disintegrates into grains of sand.

ATLANTIC MOON SNAIL. Also called Shark's Eye, the Atlantic Moon Snail is a medium-sized, smooth shell whose base is lighter in color than the purple-tinted spire. The shell is wider than it is high in most cases. 3''

COMMON BABY'S EAR. This medium-sized, very flat shell has a large, white *aperture*. The top of the whorl has many fine, spiral threads. These are quite common on southeastern beaches. 1''

MILK MOON SNAIL. The smooth, glossy, thick shell has a thickened edge along one side of aperture wall. 1''

SOUTHERN MINIATURE NATICA. A very small, thin, glossy shell whose whitish *callus* almost seals its *umbilicus*. The body whorl is not wider than length of snail. 0.3''

Top picture: Atlantic Moon Snail collars; notice top collar section shows underside of collar with egg capsules visible. Bottom picture: 1., 2., and 3. are Atlantic Moon Snails 4. Underside of moon snail 5., 6., 7., and 8. are Common Baby's Ears in a variety of colors and sizes; notice flatness of baby's ears as compared to moon snails

PYRAM SHELL

Pyram Shells are tubular with a high, pointed *spire* and small *aperture*. They are difficult to identify because of their tiny size and their similarity.

CRENATE PYRAM. This small, thin, glossy shell has flat-sided *whorls* and deeply-channeled sutures. If it is not badly eroded, its color is mottled tannish-white. 0.5"

DALL'S TURBONILLE. This small shell is long and slender with about 18 sturdy, rounded, axial ribs on the body whorl. Whorls have no spiral lines. 12mm.

INTERRUPTED TURBONILLE. This very small, slender shell has 20-24 smooth, rounded, axial ribs cut with 11-14 spiral lines. 6mm.

MARGINELLA

Margin shells are small, shiny and usually colorful. They have a narrow aperture, and the outer lip has a thick *margin*. As with the olive shell, the *mantle* covers the shell when the snail is crawling, thus preserving the shiny exterior.

GOLD-LINED MARGINELLA. This pear-shaped shell has a high spire and thick, outer lip with 4 small teeth. The body whorl has 2 narrow, orangish, spiral bands. 0.2"

ORANGE-BANDED MARGINELLA. The elongate white shell usually has 4 orangish, spiral bands. The spire is short but the aperture is wide at the base. The *columella* has 3-4, diagonal teeth. 0.4"

TEARDROP MARGINELLA. This very small shell has a glossy, white exterior and thickened outer lip. The shell lacks a spire because the narrow aperture extends upwards past the *apex*. It has 3-4, diagonal folds on the columella. 0.1"

COMMON ATLANTIC MARGINELLA. This is a solid, glossy shell with a low spire and an enlarged body whorl. It has 2-3 brownish spots on outer lip. 0.3"

CONCH

Conchs are large heavy, solid shells with a large *body whorl* and a pointed *spire*. The last two whorls of the pointed spire have rows of spines. The enlarged outer lip has a rounded *"stromboid" notch* on the lower end.

FLORIDA FIGHTING CONCH. This "true" conch has about 7 whorls with a dark brown interior. The outer lip slopes downward and the spines on the spire are short. Because immature specimens lack the enlarged lip, they resemble cone shells. The exterior is usually mottled with orange or purple splotches. 3"

HORSE AND TULIP CONCH

Horse and Tulip Conchs are moderate to very large, thick, spindle-shaped shells. They have a well-developed *siphonal canal* and feed on *bivalves* and other snails.

FLORIDA HORSE CONCH. Officially designated as the Florida state shell, the Horse Conch is one of the largest living *gastropods.* Overcollecting has made the giant, 2-foot specimens almost impossible to find. The whorls are usually knobbed. Immature specimens are orange; older shells are grayish-white to salmon-colored. The whorls on the spire have triangular knobs and the long, siphonal canal is slightly twisted. They are probably the most voracious gastropod. 18"

TRUE TULIP. This is a variable-colored shell with two or three, crinkled threads running parallel to the *suture* line. 4"

BANDED TULIP. This tan shell has narrow, brown spiral lines and smooth whorls. The tip of the siphonal canal is sometimes tinted with orange. 3"

WHELK

Whelks are very large, heavy, elongated shells with a large *body whorl*. Some Whelks, referred to as *dextral*, coil clockwise and have their *apertures* open on the righthand side. Others, referred to as *sinistral*, coil counterclockwise and have their apertures open on the lefthand side. Whelks usually feed on clams. The female lays long strips of egg cases with 10-100 tiny eggs sealed in each.

Whelks are often mistakenly referred to as conchs. However, true conchs belong to a different family of *mollusks* of which the Florida Fighting Conch is the only member likely to be found in the area covered by this book. (See page 69.)

LIGHTNING WHELK. This sinistral whelk has axial brown streaks and a body whorl which narrows to a long, open canal. It has small knobs on the shoulder. 6''

KNOBBED WHELK. This is a dextral whelk with rather large knobs on the shoulders. The oval aperture is cream to brick-red color and the shell *sutures* are shallow. The living animal is America's largest salt water snail. Its egg cases have a thick edge like a coin or pill box. 8''

KIENER'S WHELK. This heavy shell has strong spines on its large body whorl. The body whorl has a swelling around the lower middle. The exterior is glossy grayish white to grayish brown and the aperture is reddish-orange. 5''

PEAR WHELK. The flesh-colored shell is streaked with reddish-brown. It has smooth, rounded shoulders with a v-shaped suture channel and an elongated *siphonal canal*. 5''

CHANNELED WHELK. This is a pear-shaped, thin shell with a broad, deeply channeled suture and an inflated, yellow-brown aperture. The outer lip is thin and the body whorl is quite prominent. The thin-edged, sand-colored, egg case is shaped like a change purse, about the size of a nickel. 7''

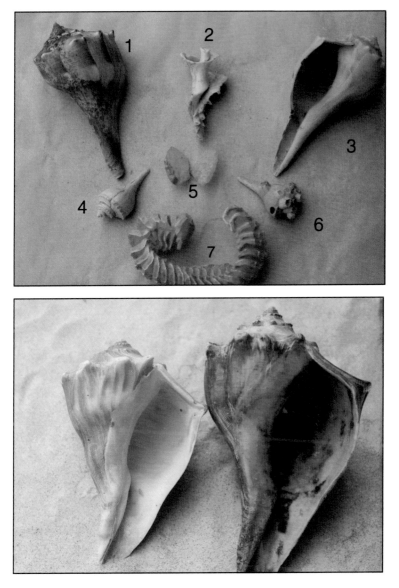

Top: 1. Lightning Whelk from rear; notice brown streaks 2. eroded whelk showing *columella* 3. Lightning Whelk from *aperture* side; notice aperture is *sinistral* 4. Pear Whelk 5. Two Knobbed Whelk egg cases detached from string 6. Channeled Whelk 7. Knobbed Whelk egg case string Bottom: Left, Kierner's Whelk; notice swelling around lower middle; Right, Knobbed Whelk

SMALL WHELK

Like their larger cousins, small whelks have a well-defined *siphonal canal*, but in these species the canals are quite short. They are scavengers and prey on *bivalves*.

TINTED CANTHARUS. This shell has a small canal with a tooth at the upper end of the *aperture* and a thick, outer lip. The spire is pointed but not elongated. The *body whorl* has dark, spiral stripes. It is found in *intertidal* weeds. 1"

FALSE DRILL. The shell has a wavy, outer lip with a single, small fold at the base of the *columella*. It has 8-9 radial ribs on the last should whorl and weak, spiral threads. It is found in intertidal weeds. 1"

OYSTER DRILL

Oyster Drills are small, rock dwellers which drill holes in shells of bivalves. They can destroy whole commercial beds of oysters. They have short siphonal canals and rounded body whorls.

ATLANTIC OYSTER DRILL. The body whorl has 9-12, rounded, convex, axial ribs crossed by many spiral threads. The *spire* is elevated. The outer lip is sometimes thickened with 2-6 small, whitish teeth.

THICK-LIPPED DRILL. This is a solid shell with an almost-closed, siphonal canal. It has broad, radial ribs and small, spiral threads. The outer lip has 4-6 small teeth. 0.7"

DOGWINKLE

Dogwinkles are *gastropods* that live on rocky shores such as near Marineland in Florida. They congregate in tidal pools on the lee side of the large rocks.

FLORIDA ROCK SHELL. The shell of this dogwinkle has a chaneled *suture* and its columella is straight and colored light orange. 1"

Top Left: Atlantic Oyster Drill; eroded.   Top Right: Tinted
Cantharus; eroded and missing the spire and small tooth.   Bottom:
Florida Rock Shell.

PERIWINKLE

Periwinkles are small, conical shells. These *gastropods* feed on microscopic *algae* and leave a mucus trail to identify their routes. Their native habitat is around rocks and pilings and in marshy areas. Some species are able to live for long periods out of water. Few of the species are common in the southeast.

MARSH PERIWINKLE. The shell of this periwinkle is usually grayish with reddish-brown streaks on the spiral cords. The *columella* is also orangy-brown. 1"

OLIVE SHELL

Olive shells are elongated, cylindrical shells which are smooth and highly glossy. They have a large *body whorl*, a small, conical *spire*, and numerous fine wrinkles and folds on the columella. They dig fast and deep, leaving a trough in the sand or a narrow "mole-like" tunnel. The foot and *mantle* partially envelop the shell when they burrow, thus protecting the shell from the erosive power of sand.

LETTERED OLIVE. A moderately large shell, the Lettered Olive has a surface heavily marked with reddish-brown, zigzag lines. The sides of the *whorls* are slightly *concave*. 2.5"

VARIABLE OLIVELLA. This is a small, stubby shell with a strong, glossy *callus* on columellar wall. It has fine, axial stripes on body whorl. 0.4"

RICE OLIVELLA. This light-colored, slender shell is often flecked with brown. The upper whorls are sometimes white to blue. The columellar wall has fine folds. 0.3"

WEST INDIAN OLIVELLA. This white shell has orange-brown markings and the spire is sharply pointed. 1"

NETTED OLIVE. Similar to the Lettered Olive, the Netted is a moderately large shell with a pattern of purplish-brown, net-like lines and dark bands on the body whorl. The body whorl is more *convex* than Lettered Olive's. 2"

Five shells on the perimeter are Lettered Olive Shells.   Center:
Marsh Periwinkle.   Partial shell at the bottom is the lower body
whorl and *siphonal canal* of a Giant Atlantic Murex.

MUREX

Murex are large, strong, spiny shells which usually have a long *siphonal canal*. They prey on other snails, *bivalves* and freshly-killed sea animals and can be found feeding in oyster beds. Adults congregate in shallow water in early summer to lay their eggs under protective rocks and ledges. A gland in the *mantle* of most species produces a yellowish fluid which turns purple when exposed to sunlight. The Phoenicians and early Romans used this fluid to dye royal robes.

GIANT ATLANTIC MUREX. This heavy shell has many short, stout spines extending from large, thin radial ribs. 5" (See color plate, page 75)

ROSE MUREX. Their color varies from cream to pink to reddish. The long siphonal canal is almost closed. The *whorls* have several large, rounded, axial ribs with 3 small axial ribs in between. 1.5"

APPLE MUREX. This shell does not have long spines but many thick, rounded, spiral cords and brown bands and markings. The short siphonal canal curves backwards and the wall of the inner lip has a dark brown spot at the upper end. 2.5"

MINOR MUREX AND DRUPE

Minor Murexes are much smaller then their murex cousins. They congregate along rocky shores or hide in crevices or under seaweed. They produce small amounts of purple dye.

PITTED MUREX. This is a rough, stout, pitted shell with 5-7 blunt, radial ribs and a definite shoulder. It has a short, upturned siphonal canal. This shell develops a squat and roundish shape when growing on oyster beds, but it becomes more elongate with more delicate spines when growing in deep water. 0.7"

BLACKBERRY DRUPE. The shell is studded with round, black beads and has a sharp-pointed *apex*. The *aperture* is purplish-black and the outer lip has 4-5 lighter teeth. 0.5"

TRITON

Tritons are heavy, rugged shells which usually have teeth or folds on both inner lips of the *aperture* and have a long *siphonal canal* at the base. Worldwide, the larger varieties have been used as horns since prehistoric times. For this, a small hole is drilled in the side of the *spire* which produces a trumpet-like sound when air is forced through the shell. In southeastern waters, common tritons are a smaller variety.

ATLANTIC HAIRY TRITON. This shell is named for the thick, hairy *periostracum* on the living *mollusk*. The aperture is bordered with small, white teeth on a reddish background. The surface has irregular *beading*. 3"

FLORIDA DISTORSIO. The shell has very coarse cross-hatching and the outer lip is strongly toothed. The inner lip is covered with glazed bumps. The entire shell is somewhat distorted. 2.5"

DOVE SHELL

Dove shells number approximately 400 species world wide and about 50 in North American waters. Though all are quite small, they vary from *ovate* to elongate in shape, smooth or sculptured, and can have high pointed or low spires.

GREEDY DOVE SHELL. The shell has about a dozen smooth ribs on upper half of each *whorl* with spiral threads on the base of the body whorl. Spire is elevated with *apex pointed*. Inner lip has several weak teeth. 0.4"

WELL-RIBBED DOVE SHELL. The shell has about 20 radial ribs on each whorl with spiral lines between the ribs. Spire is elevated with apex pointed. 0.4"

AUGER SHELL

Augur shells are long, slender and have many *whorls*. Like cones, augers have a poison gland and a harpoon-like *radular* tooth for feeding on marine worms.

ATLANTIC AUGER. This moderately-large, gray or brown, shiny shell has about 14 whorls. Each whorl has from 20-25 axial ribs. Small, spiral lines show between the ribs on lower portions of each whorl. No venomous sting has ever been reported from the poisonous gland. 1.5"

GRAY ATLANTIC AUGER. This is a slender shell with flat-sided whorls. Each whorl has 45-50 small, slightly raised riblets on the upper portion. Other features include numerous rows of very fine, spiral lines on shell surface and a small sperture. It is cream-colored, grayish-tan or bluish-brown. 1"

FINE-RIBBED AUGER. This small and slender shell has about 15 whorls. Each whorl has numerous, fine, axial ribs crossed by cut, spiral lines. 0.5"

TUSK SHELL

Tusk Shells are long, thin and tubular and open at both ends. The narrow end sticks out of the sand and is used to draw in and expel water while the burrowing foot extends from the broad end.

IVORY TUSK. This thin, gently-curved, glossy shell is usually white but sometimes has a pinkish or yellowish tint. The narrow end has a very thin slit and numerous fine scratches. 2"

PANELLED TUSK. This is a dull white shell with 9-12 main ribs with fine lines between them. The *anterior* end is smoother than the *posterior end.* 2"

CAROLINA CADULUS. This glossy shell is swollen in the middle. The *apex* has 4 shallow slits. 0.5"

Top picture: live mollusk extending its foot and tentacles from a Gray Atlantic Auger. Bottom picture: 1, 3, 5 and 7, Ivory Tusk Shells. 2 and 6, Gray Atlantic Auger Shells. 4 and 8, Atlantic Auger Shells.

TURRITELLA AND WORM SHELL

Turrets and worm shells are both long and slender but turrets are tightly coiled and worm shells are loosely coiled.

KNORR'S WORM-SHELL. The top *spire* of this long shell begins in a tight coil but *whorls* become loose spirals. The tightly-coiled top is white; the loosely-coiled section is yellowish-brown. It commonly lives in sponges. 3''

EASTERN TURRITELLA. This is a medium-sized, long slender shell which has a strong, spiral cord below the *suture* and another at the edge of the whorl. The area between the *cords* is noticeably *concave*. The color is often white splashed with brown splotches. 1''

BONNET AND HELMET SHELLS

Helmet and Bonnet Shells are large, thick shells with an enlarged, thick shield bordering the *aperture*. The outer lip is usually thick and has teeth while the inner lip usually has teeth, ridges or bumps.

SCOTCH BONNET. The whorls are spirally grooved but spiral cords are different widths, and the amount of *beading* varies. The exterior has square brown spots. The enlarged, white, inner lip has numerous pimple-like bumps. 3''

RETICULATED COWRIE-HELMET. The large, heavy body whorl has dark blotches and a criss-cross pattern of lines. The enlarged shield is heavy and smooth. 2''

QUEEN HELMET. This is one of the largest helmet shells. The *body whorl* is large and has triangular knobs on the shoulder. The large, thick shield and broad, outer lip are pale brown or salmon-colored. The inner side of the outer lip has 10-12 teeth. 12"

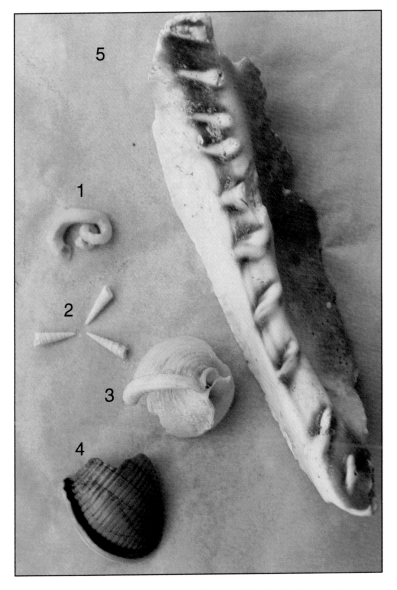

1. Knorr's Worm Shell, eroded 2. Eastern Turitella Shells 3. and 4. Fragments of Scotch Bonnet showing spiral cords and flange that shows on the exterior (back side) of the aperture 5. Fragment of Queen Helmet showing teeth from inner portion of the outer lip

NASSA

Nassa Mud Snails are small *mollusks* which may be smooth or sculptured, but the *spire* is pointed, has 6 *whorls* and the *siphonal canal* is open in all species. Unlike most marine snails, Nassas are attracted to light and have a marvelous sense of smell.

EASTERN MUD NASSA.   The shell has rounded whorls with flattened *beads* or spiral ridges. Inner lip of the *aperture* is thickly glazed with purplish-brown color. 0.8"

COMMON EASTERN NASSA. This snail has a thickly glazed inner lip and about 12 coarsely-beaded axial ribs. Spiral threads are weak. 0.5"

VARIABLE NASSA.   This shell has shoulders with 8-12 axial ribs per whorl. The color is usually light brown with white markings or bands. 0.5"

SHARP-KNOBBED NASSA. This shell has a shiny surface and a pointed spire and numerous small, pointed beads. Sometimes it has very fine brown spiral lines. Small folds appear at the shell bottom, left of the aperture. Outer lip bends over onto body whorl at top of aperture. 0.2-0.4"

WENTLETRAP

There are over 200 species of wentletraps which are quite similar in appearance.   To distinguish one from another, it is necessary to observe differences in number and shape of axial ribs, angle of the spire, and shell structure. Most of the species are white.

ANGULATE WENTLETRAP.   This small, glossy white shell has 9-10, thin ribs which angle from shoulder to *suture*. 0.9"

BROWN-BANDED WENTLETRAP.   This is a small shell with very rounded whorls. All whorls have brown, spiral bands with two bands on the body whorl. The whorls have 12-18 weak to strong ribs. 0.5"

HUMPHREY'S WENTLETRAP.   This small, thick, solid shell has 8-9, well-developed ribs, very heavy on the body whorl.   The ribs usually angle from shoulder to suture. 0.6"

Top and bottom shells are Eastern Mud Nassa Shells. Small shell
in the middle is Angulate Wentletrap.

HORN SHELL AND CERITH

Horn shells are medium-sized, somewhat elongated shells with many *whorls*. They are usually dull-colored. Ceriths are also medium-sized but have a more pointed *apex* and larger lower whorls than the horn shell.

LADDER HORN SHELL. This is a somewhat dark shell with numerous whitish spiral bands. The axial ribs are coarse and the base of the shell has six to eight well-defined, spiral ridges. 1"

FLORIDA CERITH. The whorls have several beaded, *spiral cords*. Between the cords are fine, spiral threads. 1"

KEYHOLE LIMPET

Keyhole Limpets are cone-shaped shells with an oval-shaped base. In young limpets, there is a slit in the shell on the *anterior* edge of the shell. As the shell grows, the slit is filled in and in adults becomes a hole at the shell's *apex*. This hole is used to expel wastes and water. Most Keyhole Limpets are vegetarians which feed on *algae*-covered rocks at night.

LISTER'S KEYHOLE LIMPET. This small shell has prominent, sometimes scaly, radial ribs which form a rough exterior. Every fourth rib is sometimes larger. Concentric threads form little squares where they cross the ribs. 1"

CAYENNE KEYHOLE LIMPET. This very small shell has a hole just below the apex. The shell has numerous, irregular radial ribs, every third or fourth rib being larger. The interior is usually gray or whitish. 0.7"

Chapter Four

Top Gun To The Rescue

The invader came to wreck his havoc
In this our happy flock,
He dove on his prey
Where they innocently lay
But Top Gun just cleaned his clock.

Shells aren't only pretty -- they're great protection.
If we'd had shells, Imogene Myrtle and I wouldn't have
needed Top Gun to come to our rescue one time when we
were almost kidnapped.

It happened when I was just a few weeks old, still naked, I'd guess you say, in the nest. You know, no real feathers yet.

Mom said she wanted to check on the baby hatchlings in the nest down the way. Both their mom and dad had been away for a while and you just can't leave baby pelicans for long without somebody to keep them warm. You might not know this, but baby pelicans don't have any way to keep themselves warm until they have feathers to do it for them.

Mom looked around real good, craned her head up, studying the sky and the treetops. Everything looked safe, she thought. So she flew down there, figurin' to only be gone a few minutes. Dad had been out fishing since lunch.

Me and my sister Imogene were just kinda looking around, hoping to see Dad coming back with some dinner.

Well, it all happened so quick, I'm not real clear on it all. The first thing I noticed was like a shadow over the nest. It wasn't so big at first, but then it just grew.

I looked up and it looked like a huge monster, the Darth Vader of birds, headed our way, feet first. Dad said later my reflexes must have taken over, because I jumped on top of Imogene and ducked my head.

And before I even had time to think about what was going to happen next, I heard a kind of "swoosh" sound and then a loud "awwwwk, awwwwk," and then I did look up.

"...a huge monster, headed our way, feet first."

And like I said before, it was awesome. That giant bird (turned out to be a hawk) was floppin' on the ground with blood coming out of his chest.

My Dad had dived in, Top Gun to the rescue, my Mom said later. He angled in toward our nest and then, with just astounding wing power, pulled himself up into a steep takeoff position, came up under that hawk who was diving, and hit him in the chest with the hooked end of his beak. Knocked that hawk for a fare-the-well, too!

Well, the hawk was dazed and flopped around a bit, then flew away, kinda limply. I have a feeling he won't be comin' around here any more.

Dad had a mighty sore neck for a week...

He told me he he was proud of my reflexes.

Chapter Five

Beach Birds

Whereas most marine life is hidden from the casual observer, creating the illusion of the beach as a tranquil world, birds bring soaring, diving, often frantic activity to the shore. From their raucous screeches as they wheel over the sea to their hippity-hops along the sand as they probe for food -- they are evidence there is much life close by.

Though some waders are pretty casual about human intruders, it is difficult to get very close to most beach birds. For this reason, identification depends upon prominent, physical characteristics: profile of the bird when flying, shape of tail, bill and wing, and color. Binoculars will make bird identification easier but they are not critical.

Note: A bird's color is not always a reliable identifying factor. Confusion can stem from the fact that a juvenile bird's plumage is not the same color as an adult's and many birds change their colors according to the season.

Probe-like   Decurved   Spear

These three bill-shapes are commonly found in water and shore birds. The probe-like shape indicates a bird like the sandpiper which forages for its food by probing into soft ground or feeding in deep water. The whimbrel uses its decurved bill to probe for and feed on aquatic organisms in water as well as in soft ground. The spear shape is more common on terns to allow them to grasp or impale small fish or other aquatic life on the ground or in shallow pools.

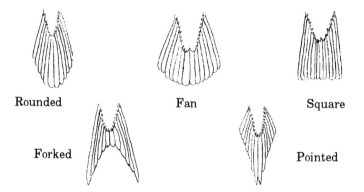

Rounded   Fan   Square

Forked   Pointed

For birds, tail shape is important aerodynamically. The forked tail, as found on some terns, offers the finest control. The rounded, fan-shaped and square tails are more "general-purpose" in nature. And the pointed tail acts as little more than a rudder for birds like the gannet.

SHOREBIRDS

Shorebirds, sometimes called waders, flit and strut the beach in all seasons. There are two major subdivisions based primarily on the bill shape: plovers and sandpipers. Plovers and their kin have short, stubby bills for picking up animal life directly from the beach. Sandpipers and their kin have long, needle-like bills for feeding in deep water and picking up marine insects and other small marine life.

MARBLED GODWIT. One of the largest shorebirds, he is the only one with an upturned bill and no white in the plumage. He is distinguished by buff brown and black markings. The pointed bill tip is black, and the legs blue-gray. In flight he shows a patch of cinnamon on the upper wing and entire undersurface. He is found fall and winter on coastal areas of south. 18"

WHIMBREL. Otherwise known as the common curlew, the Whimbrel has prominent brown and white head stripes, a gray-brown body and blue-gray legs. He has a long, blackish-brown, downwardly-curved bill and, when feeding, probes frequently. Crabs are a favorite food. Whimbrels fly steadily, high over land, in flocks like ducks or in long lines low over water. They winter on the south Atlantic coast north to North Carolina. 17"

SEMIPALMATED SANDPIPER. This is the most numerous shore bird and the smallest seen in any great numbers. A small, stable wader, he has black legs and substantial webbing between the toes. The black bill is not obviously drooped at the tip. He has slate-gray legs and is streaked gray-brown above, slightly browner in spring. The breast is ashy-white with lighter streaks. He is often seen standing or hopping on one leg or dashing about feeding with head down. In flight, flocks gracefullly turn and twist in unison. At high tide they rest higher up the beach in groups behind a shelter or facing the wind. They are commonly found in spring, summer and fall. 7"

WESTERN SANDPIPER. This sandpiper is difficult to distinguish from the Semipalmated Sandpiper but his bill is longer and it has a slight droop at the tip. Also, in fall, he is somewhat paler, grayer and has better developed white stripes over the eyes. In spring, he has more red above, giving a 2-toned rusty and gray effect. He is seen most commonly on the Atlantic coast in September when migrating, often in large flocks. 6.5"

SHOREBIRDS -- Continued

SANDERLING. A smaller cousin of the Willet, this rather thickset, small wader with black, straight, pointed bill weighs only two to three ounces. In spring/summer he shows a rusty head, back and breast; in fall/winter, when he's sometimes the only bird in sight, he is our palest sandpiper and has a white wing stripe and black legs and bill. He has only 3 toes which makes him unstable in soft sand so he follows the edge of advancing and receding waves, often in small flocks. When flushed, the flock will semicircle out over the breakers and land farther up the beach. He can often be seen standing about on one leg. When probing for food, he makes lines of little holes in the sand. He nests in the extreme Arctic area. 7.5"

WILLET. This is the only plain-colored shorebird with a broad white stripe on its black wings. He is a heavy, awkward wader. The long, thick, straight bill is blackish-grey. He is grayish above and white below with numerous faint black markings. The white rump and pale tail create a striking black and white color pattern in flight. They stand alone or in pairs away from other shorebirds. They peck items from the surface or probe or stalk larger prey in the water. Their nervous disposition makes them hard to approach. They are found all year in the south. 15"

RUDDY TURNSTONE. This stocky, medium-sized, colorful wader has short orange-red legs and a short, slightly-uptilted, wedge-shaped bill. At all seasons his wings display a calico pattern with 5 prominent, white stripes; in spring/summer, wing plumage is reddish; in fall/winter, he is a much duller color, generally brownish above with white below. The bill is bent slightly to the right, making it easier to poke it under pebbles and shells, which is why the name "turnstone." Turnstones even sometimes help each other turn over a particularly heavy object. They are prodigious diggers when looking for crabs -- digging broad, shallow holes in the sand, sometimes larger than themselves. They also can swim. Large migrating flocks separate into small groups on the ground. 9"

BLACK-BELLIED PLOVER. This plover is also known as Grey Plover. When feeding, his hunched stance and sedate movements give him a characteristic dejected appearance. Bill and legs are black; in spring/summer, he is black below, mottled gray and white above; in fall/winter, he is whitish below, showing a white rump in flight. A bold white stripe on the wing is visible when the bird is in flight and he always shows a black patch under the wing. They are found singly or in small groups of other smaller plovers, turnstones and sandpipers. Very skittish, they are the first to take flight. They often feed far out on sandbars and mud flats. They can be found winter and spring on the southern coast. 12"

Top Left: Sanderling; Top Right: Willet. Middle: Ruddy Turnstone. Bottom: Black-Bellied Plovers left side of picture; Ruddy
Turnstones on right side of picture.

SHOREBIRDS -- Continued

PIPING PLOVER. This is the only pale-backed plover on the east coast. The bright, pale orange bill has a blackish tip. The legs are orange, sometimes tinged yellowish, duller on young and non-breeding birds. A single black band (sometimes incomplete) stretches across the upper breast; rump and wing stripes are white. He nervously runs on the beach probing for burrowers. He is strictly coastal in winter; seen all year in the south. 7"

WILSON'S PLOVER. This medium-sized shorebird is the largest and biggest-billed plover. He is brown above and white below with a white hindneck collar and a single, rather broad black or grey-brown breast band. His stout bill is black and legs are pinkish or pinkish-grey. He usually feeds on higher, drier parts of the beach. He is generally alert but sometimes allows close approach. They are often found in small flocks or with other small plovers. Because the eyes are adapted to night vision, they feed on the tide lines both day and night. 8"

AMERICAN OYSTERCATCHER. This large wader nests and feeds on rocky coasts and sandy or shell beaches. He is normally seen in scattered pairs or small flocks. The long, heavy red bill can wedge into the narrow gap between a mollusk's valves. He has a red eye, black head and neck and dark brown back, wings and tail. The rump and wing stripes are white. He walks sedately, wades to his belly and can swim and dive. 19"

SPOTTED SANDPIPER. The mainly dark brown bill is pointed, short and straight. Legs vary in color from grayish-olive to yellow-ochre. In spring/summer, he has big, round, black spots below; in fall/winter, he is plain white below. This solitary hunter constantly teeters tail up and down as he walks. In flight, short rapid beats of downcurved wings alternate with glides low over water. He can swim or dive from water or wing. His range includes the south in fall, winter and spring. 7.5"

DUNLIN. The spring Dunlin is the only sandpiper with a black belly. In spring, he has a reddish back but is grayish-brown above in fall. In summer, he shows a reddish back and white below with a black belly. This rather lugubrious bird has a black, long bill noticeably drooped at the tip, black legs and a rather hunched stance. These surefooted birds are rather tame and easy to approach, even when wading belly-deep looking for food. They are fast flyers, having been clocked at 110 miles per hour by an airplane pilot. They gather with gulls, plovers and turnstones. They are found on the coast in fall, winter and spring. 8.5"

TERNS

Terns are generally smaller, lighter and more stream-lined than gulls. They have sharp pointed bills which point downward in flight, long pointed wings and forked tails. Known as "sea swallows," they dive headfirst into the water for their food but swim or walk little. They usually fish close to the surf line.

CASPIAN TERN. This is the only big-crested tern with a thick, red bill. The crest is not as large as a Royal Tern's. He has a heavy body, broad wings and a slightly forked tail. In spring/summer, the cap is black; in fall/winter, the cap is mottled brown. He usually feeds singly and does not gather in large flocks as do many terns but is often seen with Ring-Billed Gulls. He makes powerful dives and flies low when fishing. This most gull-like of all terns nests on off-shore bars with gulls. 21"

GULL-BILLED TERN. This is the only southeas-tern tern with a heavy, black, gull-like bill. The plumage is white with a black cap in spring and summer and in winter the head is all white. He feeds largely on insects and some *mollusks*. 14"

COMMON TERN. This pigeon-sized tern has a deeply forked tail. In spring/summer, he has a red bill with black tip, black cap and orange-red legs; in fall/winter the white head has a black band around the back of the head from eye to eye. Large groups hover where game fish feed, acting as guides for fishermen. The Common Tern winters in the south. 14"

LEAST TERN. This smallest tern is the only one with a yellow bill, at least in summer. In spring/summer, he also shows a black cap, broken by a white crescent on the forehead, a yellow bill and yellow feet. In fall/winter, he has a dark bill and white cap. The Least Tern has a broad tail. Because of its desirable feathers, these terns were almost exterminated by hat makers but are now under protection and increasing rapidly. Sometimes their habit of nesting on sandbars has caused whole colonies to be destroyed by unusually-high tides. They can be seen hovering over shallow water looking for minnows and other marine animals. 9"

TERNS -- Continued

FORSTER'S TERN. This white tern has a pale gray back and wings. In spring/summer, he has an orange-red bill with black tip, a black cap and orange-red feet; in fall/winter, a black ear patch appears on the white head and the feet are yellowish. He uses quicker, sharper wingbeats than Common Tern and favors marshes over beaches. He is named for John Reinhold Forster, an English naturalist on Captain Cook's second Pacific voyage. 15"

ROYAL TERN. This big-crested tern has a thick orange-red bill which retains its color all year. (A Royal's bill is not as red as a Caspian's.) In spring/summer, he has a black cap and crest; in fall/winter, he has a white forehead and black crest. The tail is deeply forked. He eats more fish than crustaceans or insects and nests in large colonies. 19"

BLACK SKIMMER. Though not of the same family as the tern, the Black Skimmer is very similar. He is the only bird with a lower bill longer than the upper. His wings are very long. He is black above, white below; the bill is red at the base, black at the tip. He usually skims the water surface searching for fish with his lower beak cutting through the water. He also wades in shallow water. This is a nocturnal bird, most readily seen at dusk and dawn feeding in flocks of 5-25 birds. 18"

CORMORANT

The Cormorant is a black, snaky-necked water bird about the size of a goose. The hooked bills point upward when they are on the water and they are longer-tailed than any goose. They swim well, sometimes with only head and neck showing. They fly in ragged, V-formation flocks with necks slightly raised and dive from a height of 100' to capture fish. Although they swim and dive, their feathers are not waterproof; they can often be seen perched with feathers spread out to dry.

DOUBLE-CRESTED CORMORANT. When mature, this bird is black with an orange throat pouch and never has any white on its flanks or chin. The immature bird is brown with white breast and forebelly. 33"

Top Left: Forster's Terns; Top Right: Double-Crested Cormorant.
Bottom: Royal Terns.

PELICAN

Pelicans are large, fish-eating, water birds with oversized, pouched beaks and heavy rounded wings. The pouch is used to store captured fish while the pelican sorts through them. He then swallows the fish he decides to keep and returns to his nest. There he regurgitates the swallowed fish into his nest for his young to eat. Pelicans, which will fly up to 25 miles a day from the nest in search of food, usually fly in single-file or V-shaped lines and hang around docks and harbors. This bird is a non-migrating species.

BROWN PELICAN. This southern pelican has a very large, grayish-brown body and head usually with a white or white-striped neck. In winter, neck plumage is white. Adult pelicans are silent, lacking vocal cords. 50"

OSPREY

The osprey, whose name is derived from the Latin meaning ''bone breaker,'' is the only hawk that dives into water. He is a large bird with long, narrow, bent wings. He has dark brown above with narrow blackish bands on the tail; the white crown and underparts are marked with a black eyepatch and another black patch at the bend of the wings. The immature osprey has a dark crown. Noted for keen vision, the osprey can see a fish from a great height; he hovers 50 to 200 feet above the water with beating wings and then dives feet first for his prey which he grabs with his feet. Barbed talons on the feet have reversible toes enabling the osprey to grip up to a 1 1/2 pound fish -- half its own body weight. He carries fish with head forward to cut down wind resistance. The osprey has been known to try to take too large a fish and get pulled under the water and drowned. If he can avoid such a fate, the osprey can live well into its 20's. Ospreys mate for life. These birds have been almost totally destroyed in Western Europe. 74"

Top Left: Brown Pelican; Top Right: Diving Pelican. Bottom Left: Osprey on the wing; Bottom Right: Osprey carrying a fish back to the nest.

GULL

In the mind's eye, beaches and gulls are inseparable -- it is unusual to be long on a beach without seeing one of these long-winged, web-footed swimmers. They swim easily, and they feed on fish and refuse. Flocking together, they form large breeding colonies. Most gulls have square tails and hooked bills. They soar for long periods and often follow boats.

Gulls and terns are easily confused by the novice bird watcher. Two keys to identification are the gull's size -- usually larger than a tern's, and the gull's bills -- their hooked bills are usually heavier and point straight forward in flight.

HERRING GULL. This snow-white bird has a pale gray back and wings which have black wingtips with white spots. The bill is yellow with a red spot near the tip and its legs are flesh-colored. In winter, the head and back are streaked with brown. This is the "common gull," often referred to as "seagull." He eats *carrion*, garbage, refuse and marine animals. A hungry gull will drop *mollusks* from a height onto concrete to break open the shell to get to the animal inside. 24"

RING-BILLED GULL. This gull's silvery gray back and wings are similar to a Herring Gull's, but the black wingtips, which have white spots above, are solidly black below. The Ring-billed is also smaller than the Herring. He has yellowish legs and a yellow-green bill with a black band. He favors a diet of fish but also eats insects and will follow a plow snapping up grasshoppers and crickets from the furrows. They are found around the Atlantic coast in winter. 19"

GREAT BLACK-BACKED GULL. This is our largest gull. He has a black back and wings while the rest of its plumage is white. The yellow bill has a red spot near the tip and the legs are pinkish. His strong, slow wingbeat and soaring motion are reminiscent of the eagle. He accompanies the Herring Gull at all times of the year and they often nest together. The Black-backed Gull is usually dominant. 29"

LAUGHING GULL. This smallest common gull has dark gray back and wings. In spring/summer, he has a black head and dark red bill; in fall/winter, the head is mottled with gray and the bill is black. He often soars and catches insects in mid-air. His name comes from its call which sounds like a strident "ha-ha-ha." They spend most of the daylight hours finding food and delight in taking fish away from pelicans, even lighting on a pelican's head and reaching inside its throat pouch. They are declining in numbers, perhaps because of the increase in Herring Gulls. The Herring Gull preys on the Laughing Gull's eggs and young. 16"

Top Left: Herring Gull; Top Right: Ring-Billed Gull. Middle:
Great Black-Backed Gull; Bottom: Laughing Gull

GULL -- Continued

BONAPARTE'S GULL. This is a small, delicate gull. In fall/winter, the head and neck are white with a dark gray patch near the eye and tail and the underparts are white; in spring/summer, the head is black, and throat and feet are red. He looks somewhat like a tern in flight because the bill points downward in flight. They never dive but they sometimes suddenly sweep backwards in flight. They eat more insects than fish. They are most frequently seen on the coast in winter. They are named for Charles Lucien Bonapart, Napoleon's nephew. 13"

GANNET

The Gannet is a large, big-billed, sea bird that flies on stiff, long, pointed wings. It feeds on fish for which it dives from great heights. The coloring is brilliant white with the outer half of the wing being black. The bill is long and pointed and points downward during flight. The neck is longer than any gull's. It is usually seen off the beaches, especially during stormy weather. It flies with stiff wingbeats. Its range includes the southeast in the winter. 38"

Chapter Six

Rite of Passage I

Dedicated to the Moment of Truth
For All Birds

Night was over, I hadn't slept a wink,
Day was come, I was on the brink
Of that defining moment, do or die,
Get out of the nest and f f f f l l l l l y.

In the morning light I stood on the beach,
Stoked with food and advice
And all my parents could teach:
 Flap hard,
 Head forward,
 Into the wind,
 Don't look where you've been;

When off the ground
        Tuck your feet,
        Lower your beak,
        To stay off terra firma
        Search for the thermals,
To keep you skybound.

First try, a naughty rock
Reached out and grabbed my toe;
I tumbled over, hit my beak --
That bruised my ego.

But I tried again, and this time
I actually began to climb.
Mom was flapping and clapping her joy,
Watching her baby boy
Get into the air and stay up, too,
At least a minute I flew.

I looked back where they stood,
My Mom and Dad, and knew I could
Do this deed
Meet this need
To be free of the nest
And face life's test.

My wings were tired, but I flapped a climb,
And it felt so right this time.
I rose from the beach
And continued to reach
For more air and more height.
I tried with all my might.
And when I dared look back again,
I had left that waddling, awkward bird
On the beach, and pointing heavenward
I was a soaring, gliding, excited
      Herman Aloyius Pelican.

Chapter Seven

Beach Plant Life

Not only has animal life adapted to the harsh beach environment, but plant life has also. Salt water and air prevent most of the more familiar forms of plant life from surviving. Plants can't grow in the *intertidal* area because sea water doesn't support ground vegetation. The rest of the beach is not friendly to most plants because the salt air dries and burns most plant life. And yet, no self-respecting sand dune stands naked in the sun. A large variety of plants dots the dunes, stabilizing the sand while presenting a colorful display from spring to fall.

SAND BUR. Also known as the sand spur in parts of the south, this plant can definitely leave a lasting impression -- expecially in the bottom of your feet if you forget to wear shoes. But it is an important dune protection because its complex root system helps stabilize the dunes. The grassy plant, with its long shiny leaves, sprawls on the sand. Spiny burs with tiny, backward-pointed spines are what do the damage when they penetrate the skin. Burs are green in June but turn to tan or purple from August to October.

RAILROAD VINE. This morning glory-type plant is a low growing vine which extends itself over both primary and secondary dunes. The round leaves are thick and *succulent*. The plant flowers most of the summer with lavender or white blossoms.

SEA GRAPE. This tropical shrub or small tree has large, green, nearly-round leaves. The foliage turns attractive colors in the autumn. The reddish, grapelike fruit is edible and often made into jelly. Sea Grape will only be found in the most southern part of this range.

CAMPHORWEED. This branching plant of the aster family produces bright yellow flowers on secondary dunes and the back of primary dunes. Some species have a distinctive camphor order when leaves are crushed. Stems can stand erect in protective areas or sprawl on the dune.

SALTWORT. This succulent plant has cylindrical-shaped leaves and grows either trailing on the ground or arching and erect. At maturity, the fruit is a purplish-black color.

PRICKLEY PEAR CACTUS. Brown bristles replace most sharp spines on this cactus plant. The flattened, oval, fleshy pads sprawl on the sand. The flowers are bright yellow and the long fruit is reddish or purple. It lives in the secondary, coastal sand dunes.

SEASIDE GOLDENROD. This is an important plant for stabilizing dunes because of its complex root system. The plant grows from two to eight feet and has long, lance-shaped, fleshy leaves. Beginning in July, bright yellow flowers spray from the stem. Flowers are thickest on the upper half of the stem.

SEA ROCKET. This low-branched annual plant can live on the open beach unprotected by barrier dunes. Succulent stems and leaves allow sea rocket to retain moisture under difficult conditions. It blooms with pale blue or lavender flowers from July - September. Seed pods are rocket-shaped capsules which scatter easily. When they fall from the stem, they roll down the beach to the water. They can survive long immersion in salt water, germinating when they wash up on the beach.

Top Left: Railroad Vine; Top Right: Seagrape.   Middle: Beach
Heather.   Bottom Left: Saltwort; Bottom Right: Prickley Pear
Cactus.

SEA OATS. These are possibly the best known dune plants. They are very salt-tolerant, the front line soldiers in the war against beach erosion -- so important that most states forbid cutting sea oats. Sea oats grow to six feet tall. In summer the heavy seed heads dance and bow gracefully on their tall, erect stems. The leaves are long, becoming narrow at the point. They are found on primary and secondary dunes. A very elaborate root system accounts for its ability to hold sand. More new plants spring from the parent plant's root system than from germinating seeds.

SHORT DUNE GRASS. This is not as important a stabilizing plant as some others. The stems grow up to two feet tall and have very elongated, light blue-green leaves. The slender seed head is supported on short branches. It grows on the back side of primary dunes and on secondary dunes.

AMERICAN BEACH GRASS. The most common dune plant along the southeast coast, Beach Grass is very important as a stabilizing factor. Its roots extend over 20 feet deep beneath the sand. If the plant is covered with sand, it will send out vertical roots that produce new stems. It grows two to four feet high, has stiffer stems than sea oats, and has long, narrow leaves. It produces flowers from July - September.

CROTON. Seaside Croton is a member of the Spurge family of tall, thinly-branching, dune plants. No other dune plant resembles it even closely. The leaves are *ovate* to elliptical in shape and both the plant and the bottom surface of the leaves are covered with hair clusters.

SPANISH BAYONET (YUCCA). This is one of Mother Nature's most painful-to-the-touch plants. The 2 1/2 foot long blades are tipped with sharp spikes which penetrate the skin with ease. Though often used as ornamental plants by beach dwellers, with little encouragement they flourish on back dunes and in open, sandy spaces.

Top Left: Short Dune Grass; Top Right: Sea Oats. Bottom Left: Croton; Bottom Right: Spanish Bayonet.

I'm weary of doing things; weary of words
I want to be one with the blossoms and birds.

Edgar A. Guest
"Hunger"

Chapter Eight

Hap Is Not So Smart

It's probably because of my Mom, but I do enjoy pretty flowers -- you know, their colors and all. Once I even followed my nose into the prickly pear cactus because I wanted to see if the yellow flower smelled as pretty as it looked.

My Dad kinda fussed at me over that. But that time he was just a little mad -- nothing like the time he was full up with mad at me.

That was when me and my sister Imogene were out looking for fish -- we were pretty young and were just getting the hang of finding our own food -- you know, proving to the folks we were getting grown up and independent. *Let me tell you, we were pretty hungry 'cause we'd been flying around for hours looking for food. I'd dived seems like a hundred times and so had Imogene, but the pickins' were pretty slim.*

We were resting and I told Imogene the story about old Mr. Willy Pelican. Seems like he had gotten pretty lazy in his old age so sometimes he just flew down to the Cut Bait or Fish Shoppe there at Christen Cove and would just walk up to the door. And darned if the man inside wouldn't throw him a fish.

The more I talked about it and thought about it, it didn't seem so dumb to me. In fact, it seemed pretty smart. I told Imogene we could do it the same as Willy. I was tired and I knew Imogene was, too. Why couldn't we?

I told Imogene the story about
old Mr. Willy Pelican.

"Ah, you wouldn't dare," said Imogene. "You're too scared, and anyway, Mom and Dad would be really mad."

Well, I guess I just kind of lost my head for a minute -- I mean I was the big brother and I was inclined to show off now and then. The next thing I knew I heard myself saying I wasn't any Tweety Bird and I'd show her a thing or two. And anyway, my stomach was empty and I knew Dad would be all over my case for not being able to get any supper.

"I'm going," I said, "and if you don't want to go, I'll just go by myself."

I figured I'd shame her into coming with me. But she just circled the cove and fish store a few times and lit on a piling.

So, it was up to me and it looked harmless enough. Just to the left of the fish shop door a guy had dropped a few lines in the water. And two old geezers were playing checkers on the wooden bench just to the right of the door.

But Imogene still wasn't having any of it -- she just stood on that piling at the far end of the wharf, not moving at all.

"I'll watch from here," she said. "You go ahead if you want to, but get out of there quick if it looks like trouble."

I made one more swoop over the wharf and then came in downwind beside the checker players and landed real smooth-like in front of the door, right between them and the fisherman. They looked around but didn't seem too interested in me -- they just went on with their fishing and playing.

"This'll be a piece of cake," I thought, feeling pretty proud of myself. I turned and walked toward the door.

"Hey, Jake," yelled one of the checker players.

"You got a customer."

By now I was close enough to the door to see inside and there was a man walking toward the door. "Well, would you look at that," said the man. "These birds are getting more cocky every day. What you want, young feller? A tasty herring do or would you prefer mullet?"

Feeling more sure of myself by the minute, I actually walked inside the doorway as the man reached inside a big square box. He pulled out a good-sized mullet and was just about to toss it my way when I heard a lot of loud noises outside.

Ta-ta-ta-thump! Ta-ta-ta thump! Ta-ta-ta thump!. Something loud was coming toward me.

My wings flapped some short, quick strokes like they had a mind of their own. But I was in the doorway and it was so narrow they were hitting against the door jamb.

Ta-ta-ta thump! Ta-ta-ta thump! The noise was real close now. I tried to get myself turned around so I could get out the door. "Darn these short legs," I thought. I just couldn't move fast enough.

I managed to get my right wing through the door. But just then a kid on a bike came flying by, bumped the front edge of my wing and kept going. Ta-ta-ta thump! The bike wheels pounded over the boards of the wharf.

My heart was pounding, too, and I just wanted to get out of there. I flapped my right wing a little -- it hurt some but I kept beating the air. I headed for the front of the wharf, between the fishermen and the checker players, hoppin' and flappin'.

"Watch out, young fellow," called one of the fishermen, grabbing his line. "Don't get tang..."

The warning wasn't even out of his mouth before I felt something tugging at my left leg. I flapped harder...and then harder, but nothing much was happening. There was just this weight on my leg.

I was straining and straining. Then out of the corner of my eye I saw the fisherman reach down behind me with a knife, and all of a sudden, the weight was gone. My wing was really hurting now, but I just kept flappin'. And then I was lifting, away from the wharf, away from the fish store, away from free and easy food.

The cove was far behind me when Imogene caught up.

"Slow down," she hollered. "Are you alright?"

Well, I slowed down a bit, but all I wanted was to get home. My wing was hurting more and more and I noticed a little blood where I took the hit.   Imogene noticed it, too, about then. She moved in front of me so I could ride easy on her draft and together we limped toward Pelican Island.

There was no doubt my Dad was mad. After I explained what happened, he just gave me this stony stare, turned his back and then took off for the ocean.

I sat there and watched him fly higher than I'd ever seen him go, then dive as fast as he could. But, the crazy thing was, he didn't bring up any fish -- he just flew up again and dived again...and again...and again -- I must have counted 20 dives without stopping.

I huddled down on the ground, didn't look at Mom, just put my head down between my wings. After awhile, there he was, standing in front of me, wings drooping, but head up and eyes staring straight into mine.

"A pelican who can't get his own food is a dead pelican," he said very softly. "Get used to handouts and after awhile you'll forget how to fish and that's the beginning of the end."

Without another word, he settled down beside me and closed his eyes.

This time, Mom didn't write a poem.

Chapter Nine

A Few Crustaceans

Crustaceans are a motley lot, including true crabs on the one hand and their remote cousins the wood louse and the fairy shrimp on the other hand. A walk on the beach might well introduce you to a crustacean or two: a hermit crab peeking from a moon snail shell or some dead barnacles clinging to a piece of wood washed ashore.

Barnacles might seem more akin to *mollusks* than crabs, but though they look very different, crabs and barnacles do share some common characteristics. Unlike humans, which have an internal bone structure, crabs and barnacles have an external skeleton, called an *exoskeleton.* Both species shed their skeletons when they outgrow them and then grow new, bigger skeletons. This process is called *molting.* In fact, crustaceans, with their external skeletons and segmented bodies and multiple legs, are closely related to insects.

GHOST CRAB. These crabs get their name from their tan coloration which blends so closely with the color of the sand that they seem to appear from nowhere. They inhabit the dunes but must return to the water several times a day to wet their gills. They can be seen most readily just after sunrise and just before sunset in the dry, dune sand. Look for deep holes, as deep as 3' and the size of a golfball. Then sit and wait. **Do not** put your hand in the hole. Their *carapace* is rectangular with nearly vertical sides. Eyestalks are large and club-shaped with eyes capable of 360° vision. In fact, vision is so good they can catch insects in mid air. But they must burrow as protection from birds because they can't see overhead. Pincers are unequal in size and their strong, long, hairy, walking legs enable them to attain speeds of 10 mph. When the moon is full, they scuttle along the beach facing the moon. They help keep the beach clean of *carrion*, but they also eat beach fleas, mole crabs and just about anything smaller than themselves.

HERMIT CRAB. Though the Hermit Crab *molts,* the shell he sheds is not his own. He is called a hermit because he lives in a stolen shell. He can be discovered in shallow water *sloughs* or even occasionally in the dunes, dragging around a whelk or moon snail shell. The hermit crab has unequal claws, the right one larger than the left. It hangs on to its adopted shell with special hooks on its back legs and two well-developed walking legs enable it to drag the stolen shell. If you were ever to see one naked, without a shell, you would see an odd, elongated, shrimp-sized creature looking somewhat like a miniature lobster.

HORSESHOE CRAB. These marine oddities are not considered true crustaceans by scientists, but belong to a subphylum of antropods which includes sea spiders and scorpions. Nevertheless, they are one of the most unusual marine animals. They can be truly called a living fossil. The species is known to have lived in the seas for 300 million years; their only close relatives have been extinct for millions of years. Horseshoe crabs have a horseshoe-shaped, *convex* carapace, four eyes and a spine-like tail. Unlike true crabs, their eyes are set into the *carapace* instead of on stalks. These include 2 compound eyes on the top of the shell and 2 simple eyes in the front. Even with all this eye power, they do not register pictures, only light and dark. On the underside, behind the legs, are 6 coils of gills for respiration. A true "blue blood," the Horseshoe Crab's blood turns blue when exposed to oxygen because, like crustaceans and most *mollusks*, it has copper in its blood. Lysate, an extract from the horseshoe crab's blood, is used in cancer research and the detection of spinal meningitis. They are found in shallow water from near the low tide mark to deep water. Water currents flowing over the unusually-shaped shell tend to press the animal into the sand. To swim, which they usually do at night, they turn upside down so the flow of water will keep their shell off the ocean bottom. The spiny tail is not a weapon but a device to turn itself over. They will grow to 24'' as adults.

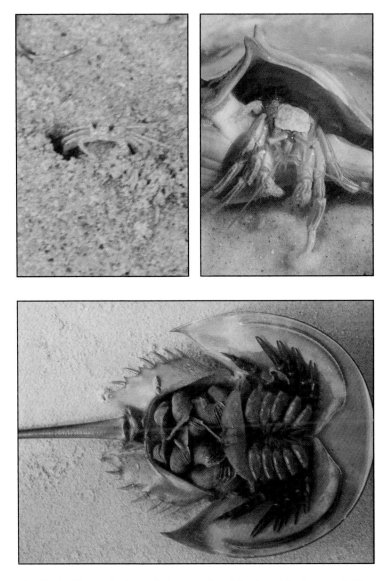

Top Left: Ghost Crab; look how well it blends with the sand; Top Right: Hermit Crab. Bottom: Horseshoe Crab.

LITTLE GRAY AND BAY BARNACLE. These very small, conical-shaped animals, with their 6 limy, overlapping plates, are very similar. Six pairs of fine, feathery legs can extend through a gap in the top two plates to catch minute food particles. Just before it reaches its adult size, and has *molted* for the last time, the barnacle attaches itself headfirst onto a hard surface: a ship's hull, dock piling, rock or even the outside of a horseshoe crab. It remains in that place for life.

PURSE CRAB. Shaped like a child's coin purse, this oval-shaped crab is beige with a variety of patterns. Notice the three spikey appendages protruding from the rear of the *carapace.* It lives just offshore and grows to 2" in diameter.

SPECKLED CRAB. The brown carapace and legs are decorated with white spots. Notice the carapace is pointed at the ends. The Speckled Crab gets to 4.5" in size and prefers tide pools.

COMMON GOOSE BARNACLE. This larger barnacle, up to six inches, has flattened, lance-shaped sides and a flexible stalk. These deepwater specimens are often found on the beach attached to driftwood or floats. They attach to objects with the purplish-brown stalk which is one-half the animal's total length.

MUD OR GHOST SHRIMP. This big-clawed, 2'' shrimp digs a U-shaped burrow in the tidal flats. It sucks in organic matter and eliminates waste pellets which can commonly be seen sprinkled around its hole.

MOLE CRAB. Not true crabs, these small, 1'' long, oval creatures have a carapace, plumed and pliant antennae, and walking legs. The mole crab always stays in the active surf zone in the summer and appears to go into deeper water in winter. Unlike true crabs, mole crabs do not have pincers and thus are harmless to pick up. The carapace is egg-shaped, grayish tan and *convex.* Also known as the Sand Bug, Mole Crabs are frequently used for bait by surf fishermen.

Top Left: Bay Barnacle; Top Right: Purse Crab. Bottom: Speckled
Crab

A fisherman fishing at Mayfair,
Hauled out a crab who said "Hey, there!"
Some things, it would seem,
Are removed from the stream
That would have done better to stay there.
Anonymous

Chapter Ten

The Last Laugh

Watching crabs always makes me laugh -- they look pretty silly, darting and scurrying sideways on the sand. Now that I think about it -- how come they're so fast running sideways and I'm so slow running straight ahead?

Oh well, maybe I'll think about that tomorrow...

Of course, when I really want to laugh, I just remember the look on Keith's face.

Keith had been a pest around our nest since I was just a chick. I mean, lots of gulls came around when Mom or Dad brought home a meal. They would flop around, begging for some fish, and Mom and Dad were usually ok with that.

But this Keith -- what a piece of work! Like daily -- sometimes twice a day -- there'd he be, squawking around -- him and his Ha Ha Hee Ha. You see he was a Laughing Gull and you could always tell it was Keith because he had this screwy laugh with a little hiccup at the end -- "Hee Ha," he'd hiccup. I called him Keith, the No-Grief Thief because he'd just swoop down, uninvited, and help himself. No doubt about it -- he had more gall than your average gull.

Mom and Dad were just too good natured to make a fuss.

But there was this one day. Imogene wasn't feeling too well, so she stayed home and I was going to bring her some food.

I was flying low over the beach when I spotted a pretty nice-looking, fresh fish just lying there. I went closer to have a look and, doggone, but it was attached to a fishing line which was attached to a piece of a pole.

"Some fisherman had some bad luck," I thought. Then I had this bright idea -- if I could just get that fish and piece of rod back to our nest.

But that was the hard part. You see, Pelicans don't fly with fish or anything else in their pouches because it's almost impossible to fly with any weight up front like that.

But I nudged this line and fish and piece of pole into a pile and got it into my pouch. Then, somehow, I had to get off the ground.

I threw my head way up, as far as I could, and flapped as hard as I could. There was a pretty stiff wind, so that helped. And it's a good thing I didn't have far to go. As it was, I had to get in behind a friend for a little lift or I wouldn't have made it even then.

When I got back to the nest, I told Imogene what I had in mind. She got so excited, she forgot she wasn't feeling so good. We arranged that fish nice and appetizing on the edge of the nest and tucked the line and piece of pole just under the edge of Imogene's wing. Then we just settled down to wait.

Of course, we didn't have to wait long. Ole Keith knew when the catch was in, and, sure enough, in a few minutes, here he came.

We pretended not to notice as he let out his "Ha Ha, Hee Ha", and dived straight for the set-up.

He grabbed that sucker fish and took off without so much as a "by-your-leave."

The line played out from under Imogene's wing and Keith didn't even notice. Then with a "swoosh," there

went the piece of pole, and that bird must have dropped 30 feet in the air. But he was still trying to hold on. It hadn't dawned on him yet what had happened.

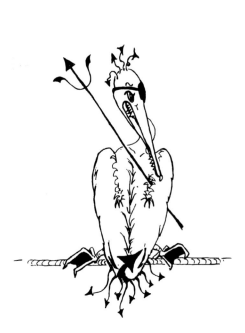

Last we saw of ole Keith that crazy gull was churnin' the air to get up 10 feet, then dropping 15 feet, then churnin' up again until he was finally out of sight.

I guess the Devil made me do it. But Imogene and I had the last laugh.

Chapter Eleven

Serendipity

Much of the excitement and pleasure of the beach comes from the unexpected, serendipity. Because the tides wash the beach clean twice each day, the *intertidal* zone is almost virgin territory each time you step out on it. Today might be the day a live anemone attached to a whelk floats ashore at your feet. Or the unusual pattern taking shape in the wet sand turns out to be a live sand dollar. Or an unusually high tide brings you some sea stars.

To come face to face with any of the creatures described below or their traces is, in many ways, to meet an "alien" life form. To touch them is to touch the world they inhabit and poses a challenge for the present while suggesting a connection to the earth's ancient past. But remember, if a specimen is still alive, observe it and then return it to its natural habitat.

SAND DOLLAR. The "true" Sand Dollar does not inhabit the southeastern coast, but its close relatives and look-alikes, the keyhole urchin and the six-hole urchin do. They live a few inches beneath the sand in crowded beds lying parallel to the shore. Storm surge and strong surf wash them ashore. Tiny tube feet in the keyholes on top are used for breathing; the tubes on the underside pass food to the central mouth and propel the sand dollar into the sand for protection.

Keyhole Urchin is almost circular and flat. It varies in color from tan to light brown to grayish. It has five slots in the upper *test* which also bears the imprint of a five-rayed star. Two pairs of slots are in line with four of the imprinted rays and the fifth is larger and between the rear slots.

Six-hole Urchin is slightly smaller than the keyhole urchin, but its upper test also bears the imprint of a five-rayed star. Five of the six slots are in-line with the imprinted rays. Its color varies from silver-gray to tan to yellowish brown.

SPIRULA SHELL. Spirula is most unique because it lives inside a marine animal rather than living independently. This shell, with its 25 to 37 gas and air-filled chambers, is created by a nautilus-like animal, Spirula, and remains inside the animal until it dies. After the animal dies, the shell floats to the surface and is commonly washed ashore. The animal itself is very rarely captured. 1''

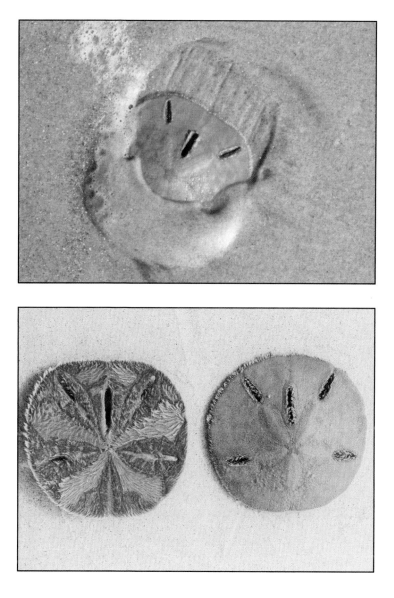

Top: Live sand dollar burrowing in the sand. Bottom: Live sand dollars; left is a view of underside showing small, tubular feet; right is a view from the top with keyholes evident; good eyes can spot the small tubes that line the inside of the inner margin of the keyholes.

SEA URCHIN. This animal is a relative of the sea star. Its dome-shape and long spines make you think of a porcupine. It moves by siphoning water through the pore on top of the dome and pumping it through tube feet on the bottom. Though it can move in any direction, in shallow waters it generally moves away from the light toward shaded or dark areas.

Atlantic Purple Sea Urchin is the most visible sea urchin on the southeastern coast. Its spines are purplish brown or reddish gray. The longest spines are near the top, but the very top is free of spines. The area around the top pore has four plates, each 1/4 of a circle.

Slate-pencil Urchin has spines which are much heavier and blunter than an Atlantic Purple Sea Urchin's. The area around the top pore has small, flattened spines.

SHARK'S TEETH. These ominous sights are numerous on many southeastern beaches because the formidible shark's mouth is armed with many rows of teeth. They are not anchored in sockets in the shark's jaw but lie in rows in the gum tissue, in some species as many as 16 rows. The outer row falls out yearly and is replaced by the next row while a new row grows behind. Since sharks have been in existence for some 200 million years or so, there are many of these tiny weapons buried in the sands of the ocean floor and the beach, and they make exciting discoveries for the beach walker.

PLUMED WORM. This phenomenon is a burrowing worm which lives in a long, deep, parchment tube which can be easily fragmented. For camouflage it weaves bits of shell, seaweed and other marine debris into its tube.

SPONGE. Though it looks like a plant, the sponge is an animal made up of individual cells which act almost independently to support the basic functions of animal life. Considered the most primitive of the many-celled animals, probably evolving more than 600 million years ago, it lives permanently attached to the ocean floor, likely subsisting on small organic particles and plankton in seawater. They have no nervous system or power of locomotion. Like the Sea Star, a sponge can regrow body parts.

SEA WHIP. This branching, "twiggy" creature looks like a plant but is actually a colony of animals of the coral family. Stems and branches are pitted with small pores. Color ranges from purple and red to yellow and tan.

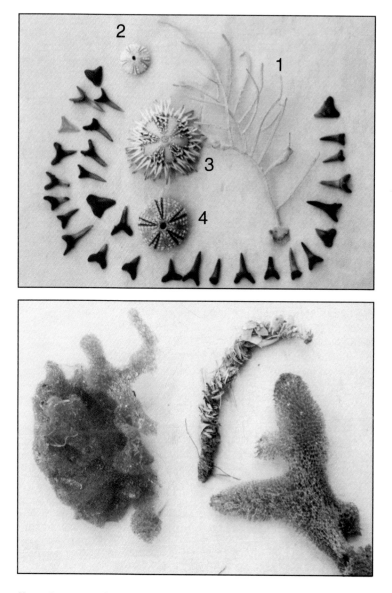

Top picture: 1. Sea Whip 2. and 4. Atlantic Purple Sea Urchin
test with spines eroded 3. Atlantic Purple Sea Urchin with spines
still intact. Bottom: Sponges on either side of a plumed worm;
notice the bits of shell and other material woven into the casing

SEA STARS.   These 5-rayed creatures are commonly called "starfish." Truly a creature of the sea, the sea star has no blood in its system, but rather has a water-vascular system and breathes through its skin and tube feet.   At the juncture of the 5 rays is the main body, a central disk which has a mouth in the center of the underside.   The Sea Star feeds by pulling on a *mollusk* to open its shell, then turning his stomach inside out and pushing into the mollusk shell, digesting the mollusk inside its own shell.   Each ray has two to four rows of tube feet on the underside which enable the sea star to crawl along the ocean bottom with an undulating movement.   A tiny red spot at the tip of each arm is sensitive to light.   The disk has the ability to regenerate any arm which has been destroyed.   Sea stars congregate in dark crevices, under or along side rocks and empty shells.

Common Sea Star is a larger sea star with blunt, thick rays and is usually tan, brown, or olive with tones of orange or red.   The spines are scattered over arms and disk, not arranged in neat rows.

Comb Starfish grows up to one foot in diameter and has marginal plates, which resemble neat stitching, bordering each arm. Their color varies from orange to mauve above, yellow below.

Dwarf Brittle Star is a very small, long-armed sea star with a 1/2" disk and 1" rays. The disk is round and plump with a white spot at the margin near the base of each ray.   This sea star is capable of emitting a luminescent light.

Cushion Star is the largest Atlantic coast sea star. Thick-bodied and highly arched, it is difficult to tell where the arms separate from the disk. The upper surface has knobby spines and raised ridges which form a network of squares and triangles. It has a very hard skeleton.

Flat Starfish is a shallow water starfish with marginal plates bordering each ray but only on the underside.   Arms are long and narrow and color varies from rosy-orange to yellowish-gray.

SKATE EGG CASES.   The skate is a wide, flat, bat-winged animal with a long tail. Dating back to the Cretaceous Age and related to the sting ray, these animals are bottom dwellers, sometimes found in shallow waters.   The female lays her eggs in little oblong black cases which often wash onto the beach after the eggs hatch. They have been referred to as "mermaids' purses" or "devils' purses."

MARTESIA WOOD BORERS.   These small, destructive mollusks belong to the same family as angel wings.   They are found world-wide in warm waters, particularly in wood and large floating seeds.

Top Left: Skate egg cases; Top Right: A piece of wood with Martesia Wood Borers embedded.   Bottom: Three sea stars; Common Sea Star on far right; middle is underside of Comb Starfish; far left is top view of Comb Starfish; notice the neat "stitching" which borders the arms on both sides of the starfish.

JELLYFISH. With over 200 species, jellyfish are a varied group of marine animals which often wash upon the beach after heavy weather and look like little more than a glob of protoplasm. In reality, their bodies combine more than 95% water with minerals and organic material to form a strong jelly-like material. Most are harmless, but some can hurt. These creatures are not antagonistic to man in particular, but stinging cells in their tentacles dangling from the underside sting anything they come into contact with. Because they are not strong enough to swim against the current, jellyfish spend their lives floating in the ocean, catching their food in their tentacles. They are not true fish -- they do not have backbone, brain, heart, blood or a nervous system. They vary in diameter from 1 inch to 7.5 feet. Fossil imprints of jellyfish have been found in 500 million-year-old rocks. There is likely no good reason to handle a jellyfish -- the best practice is to observe from a distance.

Moon Jellyfish, one of the most common jellyfish in Atlantic waters, has a 6-10" center disk with hundreds of short tentacles fringed around the margin of the saucer-shaped bell. The flattened body is usually bluish-white. Their tentacles can cause a rash.

Cannonball Jellyfish is found in the Atlantic waters, though this animal is most common in the Gulf of Mexico where it occurs in large swarms. It is about 7 inches wide, the dome is milky-bluish or yellowish and it has a pale-spotted band around the margin.

Portuguese Man-of-War is not a true jellyfish but it also floats on the surface of the sea. The blue to purplish float is air-filled rather than firm jelly and the man-of-war is not a single creature but a colony of dependent organisms. Its tentacles are as much as 60 feet long and contain one of the most powerful poisons known in the marine world. It is usually found near the Gulf Stream. The Man-of-War Mackerel swims among its tentacles acting as bait for the man-of-war's prey and receiving protection in return.

Dr. Hap's Cures
Jellyfish Stings

Mix ammonia and water 50%-50%. Add meat tenderizer if you have some and sprinkle immediately on the sting.

Portuguese Man-of-War Stings

Mix vinegar and water and make a paste with baking soda. Apply immediately.

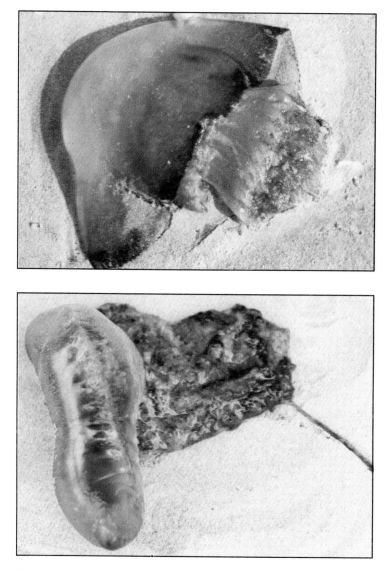

Top picture: Cannonball Jellyfish.   Bottom picture: Portuguese
Man-of-War

SEA ANEMONE. These cylindrical marine animals attach themselves to shells, rocks or other hard surfaces. When found on the beach, they appear as brown, organic lumps. But in the water they open, allowing the tentacles to "flower" from the top of the animal. As with the jellyfish, the tentacles are used to paralyze their prey. Tentacles of the pallid sea-anemone, the most common on southeastern beaches, number from 40 to 60 and are arranged in four rows.

MARINE PLANTS. Though they resemble true plants, marine plants are not true flowering plants with leaves, stems, roots and flowers. They have structures which look like plant structures but, in fact, are made up of *algae*. Most seaweeds found washed up on southeastern beaches belong to the brown algae family. Seaweeds are used in a variety of commercial enterprises: as salt substitute, in the manufacture of paints, adhesives and polishes, as a source of vitamin C, and in fertilizers.

Rockweed is a large, slippery seaweed with air bladders swelling inside the fronds. These bladders buoy the plants, allowing them the exposure to light necessary for *photosynthesis*. The type most common in northern ranges of southeastern beaches is bladder wrack.

Sargassum is a free-floating brown algae which washes ashore on southeastern beaches from the Sargasso Sea, which is located in the Atlantic Ocean south of Bermuda. Sargassum Weed is a golden brown color and has air bladders on short stalks. When free-floating in the sea, this weed is often accompanied by a community of animals -- shrimp, crabs and fish -- living within its protection. The coloration of these animals usually imitates the color of the weed. If you find clumps floating in shallow water, bring a bucket up underneath and then shake the weed into the bucket -- you may be able to capture some specimens for observation.

Phosphorescence is created by tiny unicellular plants called dinoflagellates which swim like simple animals but photosynthesize like plants. A chemical reaction in the plant cells causes flecks of light when seawater is disturbed. This phenomenon is much like a firefly's light. The light is very noticeable year round in the south. In certain bays in Puerto Rico it is reported to be so bright it can illuminate newsprint. It is more easily seen at night, especially if you agitate the water. Other dinoflagelates are responsible for the Red Tide, a toxic phenomenon that kills fish and plant life when it occurs.

Top Left: Anemone on a discarded whelk shell; out of water it remains closed; Top Right: the same Anemone under water with tentacles extended and searching for food. Bottom Left: A small piece of Sargassum weed; Bottom Right: Rockweed

LOGGERHEAD SEA TURTLE. This very large, deep-sea creature has roamed the seas for 175 million years and can grow to 9 feet and 850 pounds. It has the strongest beak of the 6 Atlantic sea turtles. At sea it is capable of swimming 25 mph, but can move only very slowly on land when it comes ashore to lay its eggs. The female will return to the beach in late spring to lay her eggs above the high tide line in a large hole she digs. The hatchlings are born at night in 2 to 3 months and begin a very dangerous trek to the ocean. While struggling across the sand, they are prey for many predators. An possibly deadlier danger is their disorientation when they first surface on the sand. Modern shoreline lights might confuse their instinct to head for the lighter sky over the ocean instead of the darker sky over land. If they head inland, they cannot reach the sea and relative safety. On beaches which are known sea turtle nesting sites, ecologists have formed beach patrols to watch for nesting turtles. If the nests are in a dangerous place, the eggs are removed and incubated artificially and the hatchlings later released into the ocean. These patrols also monitor beach nests and guide the hatchlings to the ocean.

Chapter Twelve

Rite of Passage II

Well, it's time to be off. It's been fun following you around the beach and showing you a bit of my world. I notice you've gotten pretty good at telling one ark shell from another. And I'll never forget how excited you were when you found that live anemone washed up on the beach.

You see, yesterday I turned 13 ...weeks, that is. That means it's time for me to light out for new territories -- got to leave home and start my own life. Imogene won't be far behind.

I'll still see them, I hope -- Mom and Dad and Imogene.

By the way, Dad, I know most of the time I'll be seeing the world through your 3-D glasses; but Mom, it's ok. I count on your rose-colored glasses to show me some of the most special sights.

So...
Goodbye nest,
You were the best.
Hello, world!
Today is the day,
To make my way,
Hey! Wow! Did you see that girl?

"But I reckon I got to light out for the Territory ahead of the rest..."

Mark Twain
The Adventures of Huckleberry Finn

The shore is an ancient world, for as long as there has been an earth and sea there has been this place of the meeting of land and water. Yet it is a world that keeps alive the sense of continuing creation and of the relentless drive of life. Each time that I enter it, I gain some new awareness of its beauty and its deeper meanings, sensing that intricate fabric of life by which one creature is linked with another, and each with its surroundings.

Rachel Carson
The Edge of the Sea

APPENDIX A
BEST SHELLING LOCATIONS -- SOUTHEAST

The following identifications are based on the author's success and the success of local beach combers as reported to the author.

Don't forget -- tide, sea conditions, and time of year affect the availability of shells on any given beach. Generally, beaches bordering inlets are more productive than other areas. But, in fact, any beach is capable of a surprise or two at the right time.

Beach locations are arranged geographically from north to south -- from Hatteras Island, North Carolina, to Melbourne, Florida.

NORTH CAROLINA

OUTER BANKS. Main drawback: cars and trucks are allowed to drive on most of these beaches, destroying many shells. Most success:

    a. Southern tip of Hatteras Island near Cape Hatteras lighthouse. Not in front of lighthouse, however. Try beach area accessible from beach ramp parking lot. Southern exposure.

    b. Northern end Ocracoke Island. Vehicular traffic allowed but not as heavy as in other spots.

BEAUFORT. Shackleford Banks and North and South Core Banks, part of Cape Lookout National Seashore; accessible by people ferry from ferry dock at ranger station at Harker's Island near Beaufort. Whelks, conchs, scotch bonnets, giant tuns, sunray venus among shells possible to find.

BOGUE BANKS (INCLUDES ATLANTIC BEACH AND EMERALD ISLE). An "armpit" of North Carolina where the island lies east to west with whole beach expanse facing south and affording good shelling. Especially good at far eastern end, Fort Macon. Beach driving allowed at western end.

BEAR ISLAND. Accessible by people ferry from Hammock's Beach State Park near Swansboro. North end of island facing Bogue Inlet good spot. Sand dollars, whelks, buttercup lucines.

TOPSAIL BEACH (INCLUDES SURF CITY). Both ends of island have particular promise. Southern end, called Serenity Point, also a bird nesting area from April to August. Giant cockles, olives.

WRIGHTSVILLE BEACH. Especially southern tip beyond spit of beach facing inlet. Variety of more common shells.

FT. FISHER. Rock outcroppings (only natural ones between Nags Head and Marineland, Florida) create tide pools. Live specimens (snails, hermit crabs). Fossil shells, sharks' teeth, augers, whelks.

BALD HEAD ISLAND. Private residential island only accessible by ferry from ferry dock. Beach is relatively unspoiled. Whelks, sand dollars.

OAK ISLAND (INCLUDES CASWELL AND LONG BEACH). Another of North Carolina's "armpits" which has an island lying east and west and beaches facing south. Caswell Beach is on eastern end and very good shelling: angel and turkey wings, fossil shells. Long Beach also very shelly but more garden variety.

OCEAN ISLE BEACH. Also part of armpit. Eastern end most productive. Fossil shells, large disk dosinia.

SOUTH CAROLINA

MYRTLE BEACH (STATE PARK). Myrtle Beach (the city) has many garden variety shells but beach is heavily used. The state park just south of the city offers more potential for rarer finds. Fossil sharks' teeth and bones.

HUNTINGTON BEACH (STATE PARK). Three miles of beach front. Sea stars, sea urchins.

PAWLEY'S ISLAND AND LITCHFIELD BEACH. Shelly. Mussels, oysters and more common shells.

BULL'S ISLAND. Accessible by regularly-scheduled people ferry from Cape Romain National Wildlife Refuge near McClellanville. Not heavily visited. Shelling good.

ISLE OF PALMS. North end of island most interesting. Shelly. Also lots of lug worm activity.

KIAWAH ISLAND AND SEABROOK ISLAND. Private residential and resort communities on these islands. Shelling good, especially south end Seabrook and north end of Kiaweh. Whelks, sand dollars, tellins, sunray venus.

EDISTO (STATE PARK). Good shelling, especially across small inlet at low tide approximately 1/2 mile walk north on beach. Good chance for whelk shells there.

HUNTING ISLAND (STATE PARK). Shelly. Large variety of more common shells.

HILTON HEAD. Most productive public area is at the north end of island, the end of Beach City Road. Beach fronting private residential communities on north and northeastern exposures to Port Royal Sound also productive.

FRIPP ISLAND. Private residential and resort community. Good shelling. Whelks, sand dollars, urchins.

GEORGIA

TYBEE ISLAND. Not much shelling but live sand dollars and moon snails plentiful at low tide. Parking Lot #2, north end to rock jetties on the south.

ST. SIMONS AND SEA ISLAND. Best shelling on peninsular from coast guard station northward. Access to beaches at Sea Island more difficult, but shelling generally productive, especially near beach fronting Harrington House.

JEKYLL ISLAND. Mid island, from Blackbeard's Restaurant south. Live whelks and sand dollars at low tide. North end of island at Driftwood Beach, dead trees create tide pools which house hermit crabs in variety of snail shells. Shark's teeth.

CUMBERLAND ISLAND. Only accessible by people ferry from ferry dock at St. Mary's. Good shelling of all types.

FLORIDA

NORTHEAST FLORIDA (INCLUDES FERNANDINA, AMELIA ISLAND, LITTLE TALBOT ISLAND, JACKSONVILLE BEACH, PONTE VEDRA). One of best, general shelling areas on southeastern coast for variety and plentitude. Sharks' teeth.

MARINELAND. Natural coquina rock formations on beach create tide pools which house live specimens.

NEW SMYRNA BEACH. North end facing Ponce deLeon Inlet at Ponce Inlet Park.

SEBASTIAN INLET. Shelly. Cross-sbarred venus. Note: don't miss the wood storks living and mingling with people in Long Point County Park.

APPENDIX B

CENTERS FOR FURTHER EXPLORATION

The author discovered on her travels various organizations which offer exciting programs and exhibits for beachcombers who want more. The listings below include primarily educational endeavors by various state and private organization and exclude any commercial enterprises. Listings are generally arranged geographically from north to south.

NORTH CAROLINA AQUARIUMS. There are 3 aquariums: at Roanoke Island, just west of Nags Head, at Pine Knoll Shores, near Morehead City and Atlantic Beach, at Fort Fisher, south of Wilmington near Kure Beach. Each aquarium offers its own unique exhibits and programs, and each is staffed with trained educators. The aquariums are funded by the state and in 1993, for the first time, plan to charge a small admission fee.

NORTH CAROLINA MARITIME MUSEUM. 315 Front Street, Beaufort, North Carolina. Houses an exhibit area and offers a variety of programs. Among other exhibits is the Brantley and Maxine Watson shell collection, approximately 5,000 specimens from all over the world.

MUSEUM OF COASTAL CAROLINA. Ocean Isle Beach, North Carolina. Houses educational exhibits, excellent shell collection of the very shells and fossils you are most apt to find on your walks.

SOUTH CAROLINA STATE PARKS ON THE BEACHES: MYRTLE BEACH, HUNTINGTON BEACH, EDISTO, HUNTING ISLAND. These state parks are staffed with a naturalist and offer interactive programs exploring beach subjects.

THE MUSEUM OF HILTON HEAD ISLAND. 800 Plantation Center (near the entrance to Palmetto Dunes). Offers guided walks by trained docents to explore the beaches, wildlife areas and local places of historical interest.

SKIDAWAY MARINE SCIENCE COMPLEX. Skidaway Island, between Tybee Island and downtown Savannah. Marine exhibits of local coastal significance.

DUVAL COUNTY MARINE SCIENCE CENTER. Located in Mayport, Florida. This is an instructional center, part of the local county school system. Visitors are welcome in small numbers during school hours. Several good exhibits including a comprehensive shell collection.

BIBLIOGRAPHY

Abbott, R. Tucker. *A Guide to Field Identification: Seashells of North America.* New York: Golden Press, 1986.

Amos, William H. and Stephen H. *Atlantic & Gulf Coasts.* New York: Alfred A. Knopf, 1989.

Ballentine, Todd. *Tideland Treasure.* Columbia, South Carolina: University of South Carolina Press, 1991.

Bell, C. Ritchie and Bryan J. Taylor. *Florida Wild Flowers.* Chapel Hill, North Carolina: Laurel Hill Press, 1982.

Brown, Joseph. *The Return of the Brown Pelican.* Baton Rouge and London: Louisiana State University Press, 1983.

Bull, John and Edith, and Gerald Gold. *Birds of North America: Eastern Region.* New York: Collier Books, 1985.

Carson, Rachel. *The Edge of the Sea.* London: Staples Press Limited, 1955.

Collins, Henry Hill, Jr. *Complete Field Guide to American Wildlife* New York: Harper and Row, 1959.

Coulombe, Deborah A. *The Seaside Naturalist.* New York: Prentice Hall Press, 1984.

Douglass, Jackie Leatherbury. *Peterson First Guides: Shells of North America.* Boston: Houghton Mifflin Co., 1989.

Duncan, Wilbur and Marion B. *Seaside Plants of the Gulf and Atlantic Coasts.* Washington D.C.: Smithsonian Institution Press, 1987.

Hayman, John Marchant, and Tony Prater. *Shorebirds: An Identification Guide to the Waders of the World.* Boston: Houghton Mifflin Co., 1986.

Harrison, Peter. *Seabirds: An Identification Guide.* Boston: Houghton Mifflin Co., 1983.

Tomashko, Sandra. *The Complete Collector's Guide to Shells & Shelling.* Miami, Florida: Windward Publishing Inc., 1984.

Vilas, C.N., and N.R. *Florida Marine Shells: A Guide for Collectors of Shells of the Southeastern Atlantic Coast and Gulf Coast.* Rutland, Vermont: Charles E. Tuttle Co., 1983.

Zinn, Donald. *The Handbook for Beach Strollers: from Maine to Cape Hatteras.* Chester, Connecticut: The Globe Pequot Press, 1985.

GLOSSARY

Adductor Muscle Muscles which fasten the bivalve animal to its shell.

Algae Simple plants with no vascular system such as leaves, stems or root systems.

Anterior The front part of a living bivavle shell.

Aperture The usually large opening in the last whorl of an univalve shell through which the animal extends his head and foot.

Apex Extreme top of univalve shell; the place where shell growth begins.

Axial Having to do with the midline of a body or some other structure.

Beading Raised, round knobs of various sizes on a shell's exterior.

Beak The first-formed part of a bivalve, usually above the hinge.

Bivalve A mollusk having two, joined shells or valves.

Body Whorl The last and largest turn of a spiral, univalve shell.

Byssus A secretion by certain mollusks with which they attach themselves to a firm structure.

Calcium Carbonate Mineral occuring in rocks as marble and limestone and in animals as bones, shells, teeth, etc.

Callus In gastropods, a calcareous deposit covering a portion of the shell.

Carapace The part of the exoskeleton of a higher crustacean that extends over the head and upper torso, but not the abdomen. The upper part of a turtle's shell.

Carrion Dead and decaying animal flesh.

Chondrophore A large spoon-shaped depression in the hinge line of some bivalves like surf clams.

Columella The solid pillar at the axis of a univalve shell around which the whorls revolve.

Compressed To describe a shell: flattened from side to side

Concave Hollow and curved like the inside of a circle or sphere.

Convex Curved out like a bulge on a surface.

Cord A coarse, large spiral line or thread on a shell.

Detritus Material resulting from the decomposition of dead organic matter.

Dextral Having the opening or aperture on the right side of a univalve when the shell is held with the apex up.

Ear A wing-like extension from the side of a mollusk's hinge line.

Exoskeleton External skeleton, as in crustaceans or other antropods.

Foot The underside of the mollusk's body on which the animal moves or rests when it is extended.

Garnet A hard, silicate mineral; commonly a deep-red color.

Gastropod A mollusk with a disklike organ (the foot) on the underside of the body used for locomotion.

Genera. Plural form of *genus* meaning groups of related plants or animals, each generally consisting of 2 or more species.

Hinge Top margin of a bivalve where the teeth, if present, interlock.

Intertidal The zone along the shore between high and low tide.

Magnetite An iron ore; black iron oxide.

Mantle A sheet of tissue that lines and secretes the shell of a mollusk.

Margin The boundary or periphery of a shell.

Mollusk The invertebrate scientific classification which includes gastropods, bivalves and cephalopods.

Molting A periodic shedding of the exoskeleton permitting an increase in size.

Muscle Scar Impressions on the inside of bivalve shells which indicate where the adductor muscles were attached.

Operculum A "lid" that closes an aperture in many living univalve shells when the animal is retracted into the shell.

Ovate Egg-shaped.

Pallial Line The line on the inner surface of a bivalve shell marking where the mantle was attached to the shell.

Pallial Sinus In bivalves, a shallow or deep embayment in the pallial line which marks where the siphon was attached to the shell.

Periostracum The layer or coat of fuzzy, horny material covering the outer shell.

Photosynthesis The process by which plant cells make sugar from carbon dioxide and water in the presence of chlrophyll and light.

Pigment Cell A body cell which supplies color.

Posterior   The back end of a living bivalve shell or the end through which the siphons extend.

Predator   An animal that kills other animals for food.

Radula   A ribbon-like strip of flesh coiled within the throat of a univalve which is equipped with rows of teeth on one side and used for boring into other shells and tearing out fleshy food.

Semipalmated Partially webbed.

Serrate   Notched like the edge of a saw; toothed.

Sinistral Having the opening or aperture on the left side of a univalve when the shell is held with the apex up.

Siphon   A tubular-shaped portion of the mantle which a buried mollusk extends above the sand to pass organic material into and out of its body.

Siphonal Canal   In univalves, a short or tubelike channel at the lower end of the aperture through which the siphon protrudes.

Slough   A soft, deep water hole created on the beach by scouring surf.

Spiral Sculpturing coiled around a central axis.

Stromboid Notch   A notch at the anterior end of the aperture in certain conchs.

Succulent   Having thick or fleshy and juicy leaves or stems.

Suture   Seam-like line formed where adjacent whorls of a univalve join.

Taxodant Teeth   Comb-like teeth found on a mollusk shell's hinge.

Test   The skeleton of a sea animal (i.e. sea urchin, sea star) with a stony shell and a body whose parts are arranged radially.

Umbilicus   The hollow within the axis around which the whorls of a univalve shell coil; extends from the base into the body-whorl of the univalve.

Univalve A mollusk having only one shell or valve.

Whorl   One of the turns of a spiral shell.

INDEX

NOTES